STEP-BY-STEP

Low Fat Pasta

Dried Pasta

This is a good standby that can be kept for months in an airtight container. Look for the words "semolina" on the packet, as this is top quality pasta which produces good results. Always follow the manufacturer's instructions when cooking dried pasta, and when calculating portions, remember that pasta can increase in volume as much as four times when cooked.

Anellini
Small pasta rings or tiny circles. They are good in soups and casseroles (1).

Campanelle
Twisted with frilled edges (2).

Cannelloni
Pasta tubes traditionally stuffed with a meat or cheese filling and baked in the oven (3).

Conchiglie
Pasta shells – they are smooth or ridged (rigati). The smaller shells are called conchigliette. The largest shells (conchiglioni) can be stuffed (4).

Farfalle
Pasta in bow shapes, usually with decorated edges. They are ideal for "dressing up" a plain-looking salad (5).

Fettuccine
Long, narrow ribbons of pasta made from egg pasta. They are not as wide as tagliatelle (6).

Fusillata casareccia
These twists of pasta are good with tomato sauce (7).

Fusilli
Corkscrew-shaped pasta that works well with tomato and vegetable sauces (8).

Lasagne
Wide sheets of pasta, often layered between meat and vegetable sauces and baked. Usually the lasagne has to be cooked before baking, but pre-cooked varieties are available. Dried lasagne has smooth or wavy-edged sheets (9).

Macaroni
Hollow tubes of pasta – they are often served in baked dishes with a cheese sauce (10).

Mafalda
Long wavy-edged strips of pasta (lasagnette) often eaten with soft cheeses such as ricotta (11).

Pappardelle
Wide ribbons of egg pasta occasionally with wavy edges. They are a good accompaniment to meat or creamy sauces (12).

Penne
Quills of pasta in different sizes often with diagonal cuts for catching more sauce. They are available in both smooth and ridged varieties (13).

Pipe rigati
Tubular pasta that comes either ridged (rigati) or plain (14).

Rotini
Short pasta spirals – they are versatile enough to be used in sauces or soups (15).

Spaghetti
Long, very thin sticks of pasta – a traditional favorite in tomato or oily sauces (16).

Stelline
These little pasta stars are often used in soups (17).

Tagliatelle
Long, flat strands of pasta that go well with creamy sauces. Tagliatelle verdi is green because it has had chopped spinach added to the dough. Squid-ink tagliatelle is made by coloring pasta dough with the jet-black ink from squid (18).

Ziti (rigatoni)
Good served with chunky sauces, or in baked dishes (19).

Equipment

If you are using dried or store-bought fresh pasta you will only need basic cooking equipment. But if you are making pasta dough, there are a few time-saving gadgets that are fun to use and will help you to make pasta to be proud of!

Bowls
A set of bowls in different sizes is useful for mixing and whisking pasta sauce ingredients or for making pasta dough.

Chopping board
Nylon boards are easy to clean and more hygienic for chopping and cutting.

Colander
Essential for quickly draining cooked pasta and vegetables for pasta sauces.

Cook's knife
A large cook's knife with a sharp pointed blade is essential for cutting and chopping vegetables and meat for sauces.

Flour dredger
For lightly dusting sheets of pasta or work surfaces to prevent dough from sticking.

Measuring spoons
Vital for measuring small quantities accurately.

Non-stick saucepan
Used for browning meat without additional fat, and for simmering vegetables in stock as a basis for sauces and stews.

Pasta machine or roller
A small hand-operated machine (as shown opposite) is easy to use – it will knead, roll and cut pasta. Various attachments exist for different pasta shapes. Electric pasta machines are also available, but are probably only worth the money if pasta-making is a regular hobby.

Pasta or pastry wheel
Gives an impressive-looking decorative edge if you are making ravioli or farfalle.

Pastry brush
For brushing fresh pasta with water, milk or beaten egg before sealing in a filling.

Mortar and Pestle
For pounding ingredients into a paste or powder. It is very useful for grinding pasta sauce essentials such as garlic, fresh herbs and spices.

Ravioli cutter
Round or square cutters for making individual ravioli. Pastry cutters will also give very good results.

Ravioli tray
A metal tray with hollows to make even-size ravioli. Usually sold with a small rolling pin which is used to seal the ravioli on the serrated edges.

Rolling pin
For rolling out fresh pasta dough into thin sheets. Special pasta pins can also be bought – they are long, thin pieces of wood, but an ordinary rolling pin is easier to use.

Small grater
For grating whole nutmeg and Parmesan cheese.

Vegetable knife
At least one small knife like this is essential for preparing all kinds of vegetables.

Whisk
Useful for beating eggs and combining sauces.

Wooden spoon
For stirring and thickening pasta sauces and for gently easing pasta strands into boiling water as they soften.

non-stick saucepan

whisk

bowls

cook's knife

pasta machine

strainer

flour sifter

ravioli cutter

ravioli tray

rolling pin

mortar and pestle

pastry brush

pastry wheel

measuring spoons

vegetable peeler

wooden spoon

small grater

chopping board

vegetable knife

Do we need fat in our diet?

We only need 10 g fat in our daily diet for our bodies to function properly. A totally fat-free diet would be almost impossible to achieve, since some fat is present in virtually every food.

A certain amount of essential fatty acids are necessary in our diet to help our bodies absorb vitamins A, D, E and K as they are fat-soluble and cannot be made by the body. Fat is also needed to make hormones. Recent research has proved that we all eat far too much fat. Doctors now recommend that we limit our fat intake to no more than 30% of our total daily calorie intake, even as low as 25% for a really healthy diet. Some fats in the diet are a contributory factor in heart disease and breast, prostate and colon cancers.

Types of fat in foods
Saturated fats are hard fats found in meat, most dairy products, such as butter, cream, margarine, cheeses and animal fats. Palm and coconut oil are also high in saturated fats. Saturated fats can raise the blood cholesterol level and clog up the arteries. The way we prepare and cook foods can limit the amount of saturated fat that we consume.

Polyunsaturated fats are soft fats such as sunflower, safflower, and corn oils, and fish such as mackerel, salmon or herring and nuts, seeds, cereals, lean meats and green vegetables. These fats may help to reduce our cholesterol levels.

Mono-unsaturated fats should make up most of the fat in our diet. They appear to have a protective effect and help lower cholesterol levels. Olive oil, peanut oil and avocados are all rich sources of mono-unsaturated fats.

A selection of foods containing the three main types of fat found in foods.

Eating a healthy low-fat diet

Eat a good variety of different foods every day to make sure you get all the nutrients you need.

1 Skim milk contains the same amount of calcium, protein and B vitamins as whole milk, but a fraction of the fat.

2 Low-fat yogurt, cottage cheese and ricotta cheese are all high in calcium and protein, and are good substitutes for cream.

3 Starchy foods such as rice, bread, potatoes, cereals and pasta should be eaten at every meal. These foods provide energy and some vitamins, minerals and dietary fiber.

4 Vegetables, salads and fruits should form a major part of the diet, and about 1 lb should be eaten each day.

5 Eat meat in moderation but eat plenty of fish, particularly oily fish such as mackerel, salmon, tuna, herring and sardines.

A few simple changes to a normal diet can reduce fat intake considerably. The following tips are designed to make the change to a healthier diet as easy as possible.

Meat and poultry
Red meats such as lamb, pork and beef are high in saturated fats, but chicken and turkey contain far less fat. Remove the skin before cooking and trim off any visible fat. Avoid sausages,

A selection of foods for a healthy low-fat diet.

burgers, pâtés, bacon and minced beef. Buy lean cuts of meat and skim any fat from the surface of stocks and stews.

Dairy products
Replace whole milk with skim or 1% milk and use low-fat yogurt, low-fat sour cream or ricotta cheese instead of cream. Use cream, cream cheese and hard cheeses in moderation. There are reduced-fat cheeses on the market with 14% fat content which is half the fat content of full fat cheese. Use these wherever possible.

Spreads, oils and dressings
Use butter, margarine and low-fat spreads sparingly. Try to avoid using fat and oil for cooking. If you have to use oil, choose olive, corn, sunflower, canola and peanut oils, which are low in saturates. Look out for oil-free dressings and reduced-fat mayonnaise.

Hidden fats
Muffins, cakes, pastries, snacks, chips, and processed meals all contain high proportions of fat. Get into the habit of reading food labels carefully and looking for a low-fat option.

Cooking methods
Grill, poach and steam foods whenever possible. If you do fry foods, use as little fat as possible and pat off the excess after browning, with paper towels. Make sauces and stews by first cooking the onions and garlic in a small quantity of stock, rather than frying in oil.

Fresh pasta

Sheets of lasagne, and long ribbon-like pasta – tagliarini, fettuccine and tagliatelle are most commonly found in the fresh pasta section of supermarkets or delicatessens. Manufacturers are constantly adding to their ranges and although there are many varieties of dried pasta, a wide choice of fresh pasta is now available.

Fresh pasta is not necessarily better than dried, but buying it fresh offers the opportunity to choose a ready-stuffed variety. Popular ready-filled types are ravioli, agnolotti ("little slippers"), tortellini, tortelloni and cappelletti ("little peaked hats"). Fillings include spinach and ricotta, ground beef and ham. Pasta is often made from flavored dough to complement the filling. If the filling looks quite rich, the calorie count can be kept down by combining the pasta with an uncomplicated sauce. Easier still, simply toss it in a little olive oil or low-fat margarine and sprinkle with some chopped fresh herbs.

Cooking fresh pasta usually takes much less time than for dried pasta, as fresh pasta still contains moisture. As with dried pasta, it is best to follow the cooking instructions given on the package since the ingredients may vary.

For the best fresh pasta of all, nothing beats making it yourself. Once you have mastered the technique for basic pasta dough, you can add delicious fresh ingredients like finely chopped spinach, tomato purée and herbs to the dough to give extra color and flavor.

Fresh pasta should always be stored in the fridge or freezer until ready for cooking. Make sure that you check the storage time on the package.

tagliarini

cappelletti

cheese and tomato agnolotti

mini ravioli

gemelli

fusilli

tortelloni

tortellini

tagliatelle

ravioli (small and large tomato)

egg mafaldine

Flavorings for low-fat sauces

Some ingredients seem to be made for pasta dishes. Take onions, garlic and tomatoes – three ordinary, everyday ingredients that blend easily with pasta and other ingredients to produce some extraordinarily good low-fat dishes.

To compensate for the lack of fat in the form of butter, oil, cream and full-fat cheeses, the recipes in this book make good use of the rich flavors of onions, garlic, concentrated sauces, fresh herbs and spices.

Skim milk and reduced-fat cheeses have been used wherever possible in the recipes. Remember that hard cheeses, such as Parmesan or Cheddar, are very high in fat. The wonderful strong flavor of Parmesan cheese can, however, still be enjoyed if used sparingly or handed out in a separate dish to be sprinkled or shaved on top of individual pasta portions.

Low-fat cheeses or yogurt have a fraction of the fat content of their full-fat equivalents.

Robust ingredients such as fresh chilies, fresh ginger, lemon, or wholegrain mustard can all be used to help flavour the sauces.

Dried mushrooms and sun-dried tomatoes (not the varieties preserved in olive oil) are full of concentrated flavor and add an exotic richness to a pasta sauce.

The aromatic flavors of fresh herbs such as bay leaves, parsley, basil, cilantro, oregano, rosemary and thyme add fragrance and color to pasta sauces.

thyme

red onions

purple basil

ginger

Parmesan cheese

garlic

tomatoes

dried mushrooms (porcini)

flat-leaf
parsley

rosemary

bay leaves

whole-grain
mustard

cilantro
seeds

anchovy
fillets

green chili

paprika

carbonara sauce

red chilies

salsa

pesto
sauce

lemon

tomato
purée

sun-dried
tomatoes

turmeric

fennel
seeds

TECHNIQUES

Basic Pasta Dough

Serves 3–4

INGREDIENTS
1¾ cups all-purpose flour
pinch of salt
2 eggs
2 teaspoons of cold water

Making pasta on a work surface

1 Sift the flour and salt onto a clean work surface and make a well in the center with your hand.

2 Put the eggs and water into the well. Using a fork, beat the eggs gently together, then gradually draw in the flour *from the sides, to make a thick* paste.

3 When the mixture becomes too stiff to use a fork, use your hands to mix until dough is firm. Knead the dough for about 5 minutes, until smooth. (This can be done in an electric food mixer fitted with a dough hook.) Cover with plastic wrap to prevent it drying out and leave to rest for 20–30 minutes.

Making pasta in a bowl

1 Sift the flour and salt into a glass bowl and make a well in the center. Add the eggs and water.

3 When the mixture becomes too stiff to use a fork, use your hands to mix until dough is firm. Knead the dough for 5 minutes until smooth. (This can be done in an electric food mixer fitted with a dough hook.) Cover with plastic wrap to prevent it drying out and leave to rest for 20–30 minutes.

2 Using a fork, beat the eggs gently together, then gradually draw in the flour from the sides, to make a thick paste.

VARIATIONS

TOMATO: add 4 teaspoons of concentrated tomato purée to the eggs before mixing.

SPINACH: add 4 ounces frozen spinach, thawed and squeezed of excess moisture. Moisten with the eggs, before adding to the flour.

HERB: add 3 tablespoons finely chopped fresh herbs to the eggs before mixing the dough.

WHOLE WHEAT: use 5 ounces wholemeal flour and 2 ounces plain flour. Add an extra 2 teaspoons cold water (whole wheat flour will absorb more liquid than white flour).

PAPRIKA: use 1 teaspoon ground paprika sifted with the flour.

Rolling out pasta dough by hand

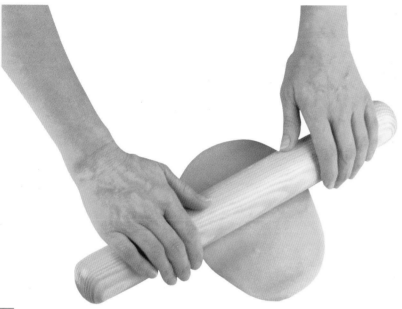

1 Cut the basic dough in quarters. Use one quarter at a time and cover the rest with plastic wrap, so it does not dry out. Flatten the dough and dust liberally with flour. Start rolling out the dough, making sure you roll it evenly.

2 As the dough becomes thinner, keep on rotating it on the work surface by gently lifting the edges with your fingers and supporting it over the rolling pin. Make sure you don't tear the dough.

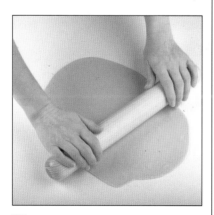

3 Continue rolling out the dough until it has reached the desired thickness, about ⅛-inch thick.

Rolling out dough using a pasta machine

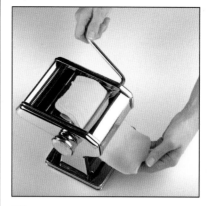

1 Cut the basic dough into quarters. Use one quarter at a time and cover the rest with plastic wrap, so it does not dry out. Flatten the dough and dust liberally with flour. Start with the machine set to roll at the thickest setting. Pass the dough through the rollers several times, dusting the dough from time to time with flour until it is smooth.

2 Fold the strip of dough into three, press the ends well together and pass through the machine again. Repeat the folding and rolling several times on each setting.

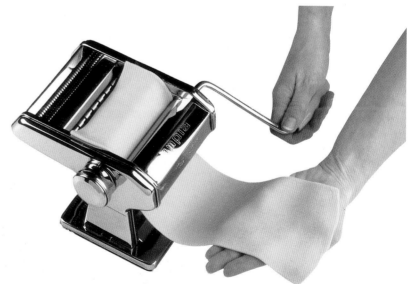

3 Guide the dough through the machine but don't pull or stretch it or the dough will tear. As the dough is worked through all the settings, it will become thinner and longer. Guide the dough over the back of your hand, as the dough is rolled out to a thin sheet. Pasta used for stuffing, such as ravioli or tortellini, should be used as soon as possible. Otherwise, lay the rolled sheets on a clean dish towel, lightly dusted with sifted flour, and leave to dry for 10 minutes before cutting. This makes it easier to cut and prevents the strands of pasta sticking together.

Cutting pasta shapes

Until you are confident at handling and shaping pasta dough, it is easier to work with small quantities. Always keep the dough well covered with plastic wrap to prevent it drying out, until you are ready to work with it.

Shaping ravioli

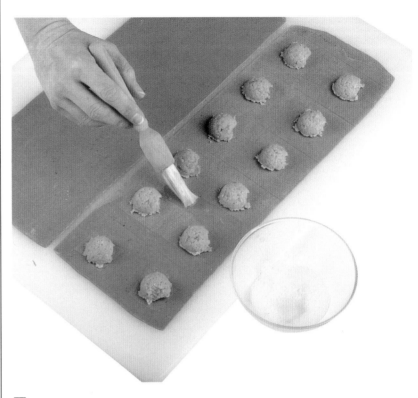

Cutting out spaghetti
To cut spaghetti, fit the appropriate attachment to the machine or move the handle to the appropriate slot. Cut the pasta sheets into 10-inch lengths and pass these through the machine. Guide the strands over the back of your hand as they appear out of the machine.

Cutting out tagliatelle
To cut tagliatelle, fit the appropriate attachment to the machine or move the handle to the appropriate slot. Cut the pasta sheets into 10-inch lengths and pass these through the machine as for spaghetti.

1 To make square ravioli, place spoonfuls of filling on a sheet of dough at intervals of 2–3 inches, leaving a 1-inch border. Brush the dough between the spoonfuls of filling with egg white.

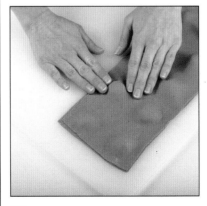

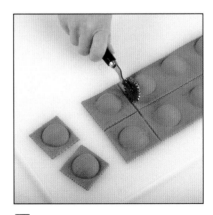

Cutting out lasagne
Take a sheet of pasta dough and cut out neat rectangles about 7 x 3 inches to make sheets of lasagne. Lay on a clean dish towel to dry.

2 Lay a second sheet of pasta carefully over the top. Press around each mound of filling, removing any air pockets.

3 Using a fluted pastry wheel or a sharp knife, cut between the filling.

Making farfalle

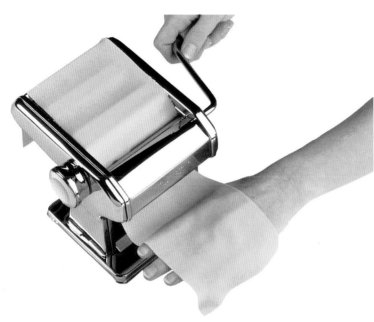

1 Roll the pasta dough through a pasta machine until the sheets are very thin. Then cut into long strips 1½-inches wide.

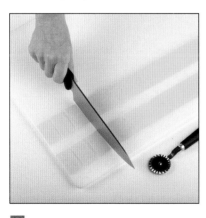

2 Cut the strips into small rectangles. Run a pastry wheel along the two shorter edges of the little rectangles – this will give the bows a decorative edge.

3 Moisten the center of the strips and using a finger and thumb, gently pinch each rectangle together in the middle to make little pasta bows.

Making tagliatelle

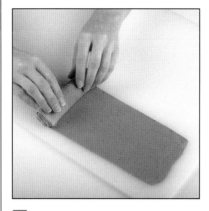

1 Lightly flour some spinach-flavored pasta dough and roll it up into a strip 12 × 4 inches.

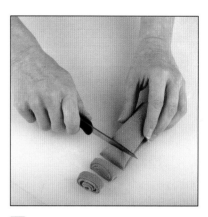

2 Using a sharp knife, cut straight across the roll.

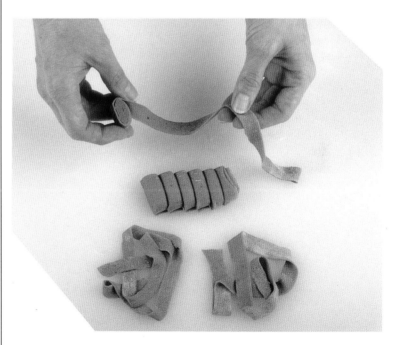

3 Carefully unravel each little roll as you cut it to make ribbons of fresh tagliatelle.

Consommé with Agnolotti

Serves 4–6

INGREDIENTS
3 ounces cooked peeled shrimp
3 ounces canned crab meat, drained
1 teaspoon fresh ginger, peeled and
  finely grated
1 tablespoon fresh white bread
  crumbs
1 teaspoon light soy sauce
1 scallion, finely chopped
1 garlic clove, crushed
1 recipe basic pasta dough
egg white, beaten
14 ounce can chicken or
  fish consommé
2 tablespoons sherry or vermouth
salt and ground black pepper
2 ounces cooked, peeled shrimp
  and fresh cilantro leaves,
  to garnish

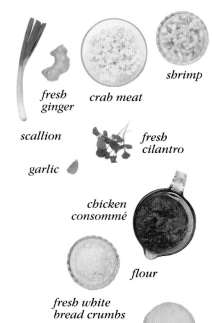

fresh ginger   *crab meat*   *shrimp*

scallion   *fresh cilantro*

garlic

chicken consommé

flour

fresh white bread crumbs

basic pasta dough

1 Put the shrimp, crab meat, ginger, bread crumbs, soy sauce, scallion, garlic and seasoning into a food processor or blender and process until smooth.

2 Roll the pasta into thin sheets. Cut out 32 rounds 2 inches in diameter, with a fluted pastry cutter.

3 Place a small teaspoon of the filling in the center of half the pasta rounds. Brush the edges of each round with egg white and place a second round on top of the filling. Pinch the edges together firmly to stop the filling from escaping.

4 Cook the pasta in a large pan of boiling, salted water for 5 minutes (cook in batches to stop them sticking together). Remove and drop into a bowl of cold water for 5 seconds before placing on a tray. (You can make these pasta shapes a day in advance. Cover with plastic wrap and store in the fridge.)

5 Heat the chicken or fish consommé in a pan with the sherry or vermouth. When piping hot, add the cooked pasta shapes and simmer for 1–2 minutes.

6 Serve in a shallow soup bowl. Garnish with extra peeled shrimp and fresh cilantro leaves.

NUTRITIONAL NOTES

PER PORTION:

ENERGY 300 calories **FAT** 4.6g
SATURATED FAT 1.1g **CHOLESTEROL** 148mg
CARBOHYDRATE 43g **FIBER** 1.7g

Chicken Stellette Soup

Serves 4–6

INGREDIENTS
3¾ cups chicken stock
1 bay leaf
4 scallions, sliced
2 ounces stellette
8 ounces button
    mushrooms, sliced
1 cooked chicken breast
⅔ cup dry white wine
1 tablespoon chopped parsley
salt and ground black pepper

stellette

white wine

chicken stock

cooked chicken breast

scallions

parsley

bay leaf

mushrooms

1 Put the stock and bay leaf into a pan and bring to a boil.

2 Add the scallions and mushrooms to the stock.

NUTRITIONAL NOTES
PER PORTION:

ENERGY 126 calories **FAT** 2.2g
SATURATED FAT 0.6g **CHOLESTEROL** 19mg
CARBOHYDRATE 11g **FIBER** 1.3g

3 Remove the skin from the chicken and slice thinly. Transfer to a plate and set aside.

4 Add the pasta to the pan, cover and simmer for 7–8 minutes. Just before serving, add the chicken, wine and parsley, heat through for 2–3 minutes.

Vegetable Minestrone with Anellini

Serves 6–8

INGREDIENTS
large pinch of saffron strands
1 onion, chopped
1 leek, sliced
1 stick celery, sliced
2 carrots, diced
2–3 garlic cloves, crushed
2½ cups chicken stock
2 x 14-ounce cans
   chopped tomatoes
½ cup frozen peas
2 ounces soup pasta (anellini)
1 teaspoon caster sugar
1 tablespoon chopped fresh parsley
1 tablespoon chopped fresh basil
salt and ground black pepper

anellini   *frozen peas*   *onion*

saffron strands   *basil*   *stock*

parsley

chopped tomatoes

carrot   *celery*

leek

garlic

1 Soak the pinch of saffron strands in 1 tablespoon boiling water. Let stand for 10 minutes.

2 Meanwhile, put the prepared onion, leek, celery, carrots and garlic into a pan. Add the chicken stock, bring to a boil, cover and simmer for 10 minutes.

NUTRITIONAL NOTES

PER PORTION:

ENERGY 87 calories **FAT** 0.7g
SATURATED FAT 0.1g **CHOLESTEROL** 0mg
CARBOHYDRATE 17g **FIBER** 3.3g

3 Add the canned tomatoes, the saffron with its liquid, and the peas. Bring back to a boil and add the anellini. Simmer for 10 minutes until tender.

4 Season with salt, pepper and sugar to taste. Stir in the chopped herbs just before serving.

Beet Soup with Ravioli

Serves 4–6

INGREDIENTS
1 recipe basic pasta dough
egg white, beaten, for brushing
flour, for dusting
1 small onion or shallot,
    finely chopped
2 garlic cloves, crushed
1 teaspoon fennel seeds
2½ cups chicken or vegetable stock
8 ounces cooked beets
2 tablespoons fresh orange juice
fennel or dill leaves, to garnish
crusty bread, to serve

FOR THE FILLING
4 ounces mushrooms,
    finely chopped
1 shallot or small onion,
    finely chopped
1–2 garlic cloves, crushed
1 teaspoon fresh thyme
1 tablespoon fresh parsley
6 tablespoons fresh white
    bread crumbs
large pinch ground nutmeg
salt and ground black pepper

1 Process all the filling ingredients in a food processor or blender.

2 Roll the pasta into thin sheets. Lay one piece over a ravioli tray and put a teaspoonful of the filling into each depression. Brush around the edges of each ravioli with egg white. Cover with another sheet of pasta and press the edges together to seal. Transfer to a floured dish towel and rest for 1 hour before cooking.

onion *orange*

mushrooms

shallot *cooked beets*

thyme *parsley*

garlic *fennel seeds* *stock*

nutmeg

dill

basic pasta dough

bread crumbs

3 Cook the ravioli in a large pan of boiling, salted water for 2 minutes. (Cook in batches to stop them from sticking together.) Remove and drop into a bowl of cold water for 5 seconds before placing on a tray. (You can make these pasta shapes a day in advance. Cover with clear film and store in the fridge.) Put the onion, garlic and fennel seeds into a pan with ⅔ cup of the stock. Bring to a boil, cover and simmer for 5 minutes until tender. Peel and finely dice the beets. (Reserve 4 tbsp for the garnish.) Add the rest to the soup with the remaining stock and bring to a boil.

4 Add the orange juice and cooked ravioli and simmer for 2 minutes. Serve in shallow soup bowls, garnished with the reserved diced beets and fennel or dill leaves. Serve hot, with some crusty bread.

<u>NUTRITIONAL NOTES</u>

PER PORTION:

ENERGY 358 calories **FAT** 4.9g
SATURATED FAT 1.0g **CHOLESTEROL** 110mg
CARBOHYDRATE 67g **FIBER** 4.3g

Corn Chowder with Conchigliette

Serves 6–8

INGREDIENTS
1 small green bell pepper
1 pound potatoes, peeled
 and diced
2 cups canned or frozen corn
1 onion, chopped
1 stick celery, chopped
bouquet garni (bay leaf, parsley and
 thyme)
2¹/₂ cups chicken stock
1¹/₄ cups skim milk
2 ounces small pasta shells
 (conchigliette)
5 ounces smoked turkey
 bacon, diced
bread sticks, to serve
salt and ground black pepper

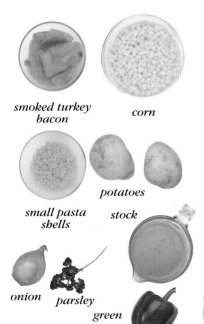

smoked turkey bacon   *corn*

potatoes

small pasta shells   *stock*

onion   *parsley*

green pepper

celery

bay leaf   *thyme*

skim milk

1 Halve the green pepper, remove the stalk and seeds. Cut into small dice, cover with boiling water and let stand for 2 minutes. Drain and rinse.

2 Put the potatoes into a saucepan with the corn, onion, celery, green pepper, bouquet garni and stock. Bring to a boil, cover and simmer for 20 minutes until tender.

3 Add the milk, and season with salt and pepper. Process half of the soup in a food processor or blender and return to the pan with the conchigliette. Simmer for 10 minutes.

4 Fry the turkey bacon quickly in a non-stick frying pan for 2–3 minutes. Stir into the soup. Serve with bread sticks.

NUTRITIONAL NOTES

PER PORTION:

ENERGY 215 calories **FAT** 1.6g
SATURATED FAT 0.3g **CHOLESTEROL** 13mg
CARBOHYDRATE 41g **FIBER** 2.8g

Pasta Bonbons

Serves 4–6

INGREDIENTS
1 quantity basic pasta dough
flour, for dusting
egg white, beaten
salt and pepper

FOR THE FILLING
1 small onion, finely chopped
1 garlic clove, crushed
²/₃ cup chicken stock
8 ounces ground turkey meat
2–3 fresh sage leaves, chopped
2 canned anchovy fillets, drained

FOR THE SAUCE
²/₃ cup chicken stock
7 ounces low-fat cream cheese
1 tablespoon lemon juice
1 teaspoon caster sugar
2 tomatoes, peeled, seeded and
    finely diced
½ purple onion, finely chopped
6 small cornichons, sliced

1 To make the filling, put the onion, garlic and stock into a pan. Bring to a boil, cover and simmer for 5 minutes until tender. Uncover and boil for about 5 minutes or until the stock is reduced to 2 tablespoons.

2 Add the ground turkey, and stir over the heat until no longer pink in color. Add the sage and anchovy fillets and season with salt and pepper. Cook uncovered for 5 minutes until all the liquid has been absorbed. Let cool.

3 Divide the pasta dough in half. Roll into thin sheets and cut into rectangles measuring 3½ × 2½ inches. Lay on a lightly floured dish towel and repeat with the remaining dough.

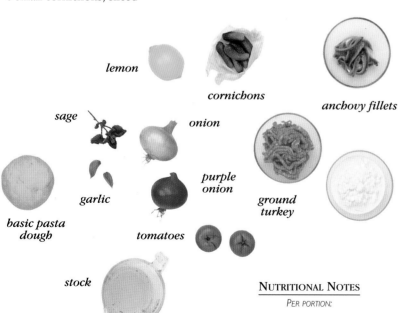

lemon

cornichons

anchovy fillets

sage

onion

garlic

purple
onion

ground
turkey

basic pasta
dough

tomatoes

stock

NUTRITIONAL NOTES

PER PORTION:

ENERGY 355 calories **FAT** 6.4g
SATURATED FAT 1.4g **CHOLESTEROL** 150mg
CARBOHYDRATE 46g **FIBER** 2.6g

4 Place a heaped teaspoon of the filling on the center of each rectangle, brush around the meat with beaten egg white and roll up the pasta, pinching in the ends. Set it aside onto a floured dish towel for 1 hour before cooking.

5 To make the sauce, put the stock, cream cheese, lemon juice and sugar into a pan. Heat gently and whisk until smooth. Add the diced tomatoes, onion and cornichons.

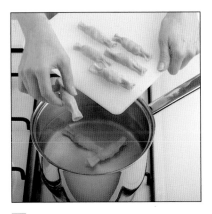

6 Cook the pasta in a large pan of boiling, salted water for 5 minutes. (Cook in batches to stop them from sticking together.) Remove with a slotted spoon, drain well and drop into the sauce. Repeat until all the bonbons are cooked. Simmer for 2–3 minutes. Serve in pasta bowls or soup plates and spoon over a little sauce.

Spinach Tagliarini with Asparagus

Serves 4–6

INGREDIENTS

2 chicken breasts, skinned
   and boned
1 tablespoon light soy sauce
2 tablespoon sherry
2 tablespoon cornstarch
8 scallions, trimmed and cut into
   1-inch diagonal slices
1–2 garlic cloves, crushed
finely grated zest of half a lemon
   and 2 tablespoons lemon juice
$^2/_3$ cup chicken stock
1 teaspoon caster sugar
8 ounces slender asparagus spears,
   cut into 3-inch lengths
1 recipe of basic pasta dough, with 4
   ounces cooked, spinach added,
   or 1 pound fresh tagliarini pasta
salt and ground black pepper

scallions

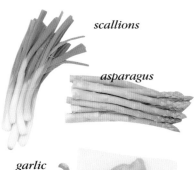

asparagus

garlic

lemon

chicken breasts

*soy
sauce*

*basic pasta
dough*

stock

1 Place the chicken breasts between two sheets of plastic wrap and flatten to a thickness of ¼-inch with a rolling pin.

2 Cut into 1-inch strips across the grain of the fillets. Put the chicken into a bowl with the soy sauce, sherry, cornstarch and seasoning. Toss to coat each piece.

NUTRITIONAL NOTES

PER PORTION:

ENERGY 369 calories **FAT** 6.9g
SATURATED FAT 1.8g **CHOLESTEROL** 142mg
CARBOHYDRATE 50g **FIBER** 3.4g

3 In a large non-stick frying pan, put the chicken, scallions, garlic and the grated lemon rind. Add the stock and bring to the boil, stirring constantly until thickened. Add the lemon juice, sugar and asparagus. Simmer for 4-5 minutes until tender.

4 Meanwhile cook the pasta in a large pan of boiling, salted water for 2–3 minutes. Drain thoroughly. Arrange on serving plates and spoon over the chicken and asparagus sauce. Serve the dish immediately.

Sweet and Sour Peppers with Bows

Serves 4–6

INGREDIENTS
1 red, 1 yellow and 1 orange pepper
1 garlic clove, crushed
2 tablespoons capers
2 tablespoons raisins
1 teaspoon wholegrain mustard
rind and juice of 1 lime
1 teaspoon honey
2 tablespoons chopped
    fresh cilantro
8 ounces pasta bows (farfalle)
salt and ground black pepper
shavings of Parmesan cheese,
    to serve (optional)

lime

raisins

red pepper

yellow pepper

cilantro

orange pepper

pasta bows

Parmesan cheese

capers

honey

garlic

1 Quarter the peppers, and remove the stalk and seeds. Put into boiling water and cook for 10–15 minutes until tender. Drain and rinse under cold water. Peel away the skin and cut the flesh into strips lengthways.

2 Put the garlic, capers, raisins, mustard, lime rind and juice, honey, cilantro and seasoning into a bowl and whisk together.

NUTRITIONAL NOTES

PER PORTION:

ENERGY 268 calories **FAT** 2.0g
SATURATED FAT 0.5g **CHOLESTEROL** 1.3mg
CARBOHYDRATE 57g **FIBER** 4.3g

3 Cook the pasta in a large pan of boiling, salted water for 10–12 minutes until tender. Drain thoroughly.

4 Return the pasta to the pan, add the reserved peppers and dressing. Heat gently and toss to mix. Transfer to a warm serving bowl. Serve with a few shavings of Parmesan cheese, if using.

Herbed Pasta Crescents

Serves 4–6

INGREDIENTS
1 recipe basic pasta dough, with 3
   tablespoons chopped fresh
   herbs added
egg white, beaten, for brushing
flour, for dusting
basil leaves, to garnish

FOR THE FILLING
8 ounces chopped frozen spinach
1 small onion, finely chopped
pinch of ground nutmeg
4 ounces low-fat cottage cheese
1 egg, beaten
1 ounce Parmesan cheese
salt and ground black pepper

FOR THE SAUCE
1¼ cups skim milk
1 ounce margarine
3 tablespoons plain flour
¼ teaspoon ground nutmeg
2 tablespoons chopped fresh herbs
   (chives, basil and parsley)

egg

low-fat cottage cheese

spinach

chives

onion

Parmesan cheese

nutmeg

parsley

basil

skim milk

basic pasta dough

margarine

1 To make the filling, put the spinach and onion into a pan, cover and cook slowly to defrost. Remove the lid and increase the heat to boil off any water. Season with salt, pepper and nutmeg. Turn the spinach into a bowl and cool slightly. Add the cottage cheese, beaten egg and Parmesan cheese.

2 Roll the herb pasta into thin sheets. Cut into 3-inch rounds with a fluted pastry cutter.

3 Place a spoonful of filling in the centre of each round. Brush the edges with egg white. Fold each in half (to make crescents). Press the edges together to seal. Transfer to a floured dish towel and let rest for 1 hour before cooking the pasta.

4 Put all the sauce ingredients (except the herbs) into a pan. With a whisk, thicken over medium heat until smooth. Season with salt, pepper and nutmeg to taste. Stir in the herbs.

5 Cook the pasta in a large pan of boiling, salted water for 3 minutes (cook in batches to stop them from sticking together). Drain thoroughly.

6 Serve the crescents on warmed serving plates and pour over the herb sauce. Garnish with basil leaves and serve at once.

NUTRITIONAL NOTES
PER PORTION:

ENERGY 421 calories **FAT** 14g
SATURATED FAT 3.8g **CHOLESTEROL** 184mg
CARBOHYDRATE 54g **FIBER** 3.6g

Lasagne

Serves 6–8

INGREDIENTS
1 large onion, chopped
2 garlic cloves, crushed
1¼ lb ground turkey meat
1 pound carton tomato sauce
1 teaspoon mixed dried herbs
8 ounces frozen leaf spinach,
    defrosted
7 ounces lasagne verde
7 ounces low-fat cottage cheese

FOR THE SAUCE
1 ounce low-fat margarine
1 ounce plain flour
1¼ cups skim milk
¼ teaspoon ground nutmeg
1 ounce grated Parmesan cheese
salt and ground black pepper
mixed greens, to serve

1 Put the onion, garlic and ground turkey into a non-stick saucepan. Brown quickly for 5 minutes, stirring with a wooden spoon to separate the pieces.

2 Add the tomato sauce, herbs and seasoning. Bring to a boil, cover and simmer for 30 minutes.

3 For the sauce: put all the sauce ingredients, except the Parmesan cheese, into a saucepan. Heat to thicken, whisking constantly until bubbling and smooth. Adjust the seasoning, add the cheese to the sauce and stir.

ground turkey   *spinach*

garlic

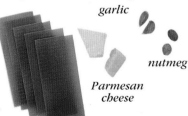

nutmeg

Parmesan cheese

lasagne verdi

skim milk

plain flour

onion

low-fat margarine

low-fat cottage cheese

tomato sauce

4 Preheat the oven to 375°F. Lay the spinach leaves on paper towels and pat dry.

5 Layer the turkey mixture, dried lasagne, cottage cheese and spinach in a 8-cup ovenproof dish, starting and ending with a layer of turkey.

6 Spoon the sauce over the top to cover and bake for 45-50 minutes or until bubbling. Serve with a mixed salad.

NUTRITIONAL NOTES
PER PORTION:

ENERGY 351 calories **FAT** 6.0g
SATURATED FAT 1.7g **CHOLESTEROL** 52mg
CARBOHYDRATE 40g **FIBER** 3g

Macaroni Cheese

Serves 4

INGREDIENTS

1 medium onion, chopped
²/₃ cup vegetable or chicken stock
1 ounce low-fat margarine
1¹/₂ ounces plain flour
¹/₄ cup skim milk
2 ounces reduced-fat Cheddar
   cheese, grated
1 teaspoon mustard
8 ounces quick-cook macaroni
4 smoked turkey bacon slices,
   cut in half
2–3 firm tomatoes, sliced
a few fresh basil leaves
1 tablespoon grated Parmesan
   cheese
salt and ground black pepper

tomatoes

onion

smoked turkey bacon

basil

Parmesan cheese

low-fat margarine

macaroni

flour

stock

skim milk

Cheddar cheese

1 Put the onion and stock into a non-stick frying pan. Bring to a boil, stirring occasionally and cook for 5–6 minutes or until the stock has reduced entirely and the onions are transparent.

2 Put the margarine, flour, milk, and seasoning into a pan and whisk together over the heat until thickened and smooth. Remove from the heat and add the cheeses, mustard and onions.

NUTRITIONAL NOTES

PER PORTION:

ENERGY 152 calories **FAT** 2.8g
SATURATED FAT 0.7g **CHOLESTEROL** 12mg
CARBOHYDRATE 23g **FIBER** 1.1g

3 Cook the macaroni in a large pan of boiling, salted water for 6 minutes or according to the instructions on the package. Drain thoroughly and stir into the sauce. Transfer the macaroni to a shallow ovenproof dish.

4 Layer the turkey bacon and tomatoes on top of the macaroni and cheese, sprinkling the basil leaves over the tomatoes. Lightly sprinkle with Parmesan cheese and broil to lightly brown the top.

Spaghetti Bolognese

Serves 8

INGREDIENTS

1 medium onion, chopped
2–3 garlic cloves, crushed
1¼ cups beef or chicken stock
1 lb extra lean ground turkey
    or beef
2 x 14 ounce cans chopped
    tomatoes
1 teaspoon dried basil
1 teaspoon dried oregano
4 tablespoons concentrated
    tomato paste
1 pound button mushrooms,
    quartered or sliced
⅔ cup red wine
1 pound spaghetti
salt and ground black pepper

garlic

mushrooms

stock

spaghetti

onion

ground turkey

red wine

chopped tomatoes

tomato paste

1 Put the chopped onion and garlic into a non-stick pan with half of the stock. Bring to a boil and cook for 5 minutes until the onions are tender and the stock is reduced completely.

2 Add the turkey or beef and cook for 5 minutes breaking the meat up with a fork. Add the tomatoes, herbs and tomato paste, bring to the boil, cover and simmer for about 1 hour.

NUTRITIONAL NOTES

PER PORTION:

ENERGY 321 calories **FAT** 4.1g
SATURATED FAT 1.3g **CHOLESTEROL** 33mg
CARBOHYDRATE 49g **FIBER** 3.7g

3 Meanwhile put the mushrooms into a non-stick pan with the wine, bring to a boil and cook for 5 minutes or until the wine has evaporated. Add the mushrooms to the meat.

4 Cook the pasta in a large pan of boiling, salted water for 8–10 minutes until tender. Drain thoroughly. Serve topped with meat sauce.

Cannelloni

Serves 4

INGREDIENTS

2 garlic cloves, crushed
2 x 14 ounce cans
   chopped tomatoes
2 teaspoons brown sugar
1 tablespoon fresh basil
1 tablespoon fresh marjoram
1 pound chopped frozen spinach
large pinch ground nutmeg
4 ounces cooked, ground lean ham
7 ounces low-fat cottage cheese
12–14 cannelloni tubes
2 ounces low-fat mozzarella
   cheese, diced
1 ounce sharp Cheddar
   cheese, grated
1 ounce fresh white bread crumbs
salt and ground black pepper
flat-leaf parsley, to garnish

1 To make the sauce put the garlic, canned tomatoes, sugar and herbs into a pan, bring to the boil and cook, uncovered, for 30 minutes, stirring occasionally, until fairly thick.

2 To make the filling put the spinach into a pan, cover and cook slowly until defrosted. Break up with a fork, then increase the heat to remove excess water. Season with salt, pepper and nutmeg. Transfer the spinach to a bowl, cool slightly, then add the ground ham and cottage cheese.

3 Pipe the filling into each tube of uncooked cannelloni. It is easiest to hold them upright with one end flat on a chopping board, while piping from the other end.

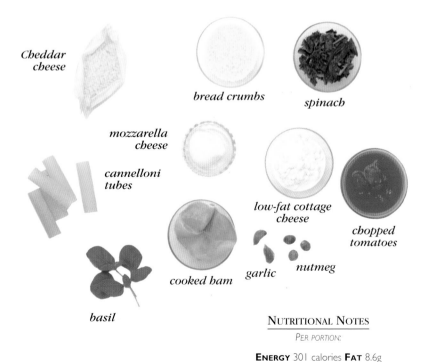

Cheddar cheese

bread crumbs

spinach

mozzarella cheese

cannelloni tubes

low-fat cottage cheese

chopped tomatoes

cooked ham

garlic

nutmeg

basil

NUTRITIONAL NOTES

PER PORTION:

ENERGY 301 calories **FAT** 8.6g
SATURATED FAT 3.6g **CHOLESTEROL** 34mg
CARBOHYDRATE 33g **FIBER** 4.7g

4 Preheat the oven to 350°F. Spoon half of the tomato sauce into the bottom of an 8-inch square ovenproof dish. Lay two rows of filled cannelloni on top of the sauce.

5 Sprinkle with the diced mozzarella and cover with the rest of the sauce.

6 Sprinkle with the Cheddar cheese and bread crumbs. Bake in a preheated oven for 30–40 minutes. Place under broiler to brown, if necessary. Garnish with flat-leaf parsley.

Ravioli with Bolognese Sauce

Serves 6

INGREDIENTS

8 ounces low-fat cottage cheese
2 tablespoons grated Parmesan
cheese, plus extra for serving
1 egg white, beaten, including extra
for brushing
¼ teaspoon ground nutmeg
1 recipe pasta dough
flour, for dusting
1 medium onion, finely chopped
1 garlic clove, crushed
⅔ cup beef stock
12 ounces extra lean ground beef
½ cup red wine
2 tablespoons tomato paste
14 ounce can chopped tomatoes
½ tsp chopped fresh rosemary
¼ tsp ground allspice
salt and ground black pepper

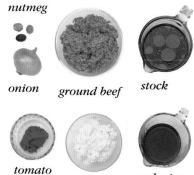

nutmeg

onion   *ground beef*   *stock*

tomato purée   *low-fat cottage cheese*   *red wine*

Parmesan cheese   *chopped tomatoes*

egg   *rosemary*   *garlic*

1 To make the filling mix the cottage cheese, grated Parmesan, egg white, seasoning and nutmeg together thoroughly.

2 Roll the pasta into thin sheets and place a small teaspoon of filling along the pasta in rows 2 inches apart.

3 Moisten between the filling with beaten egg white. Lay a second sheet of pasta lightly over the top and press between each pocket to remove any air and seal firmly.

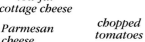

4 Cut into rounds with a fluted ravioli or pastry cutter. Transfer to a floured cloth and let rest for at least 30 minutes before cooking.

5 To make the Bolognese sauce cook the onion and garlic in the stock for 5 minutes or until all the stock is reduced. Add the beef and cook quickly to brown, breaking up the meat with a fork. Add the wine, tomato paste, chopped tomatoes, rosemary and allspice, bring to a boil and simmer for 1 hour. Adjust the seasoning to taste.

6 Cook the ravioli in a large pan of boiling, salted water for 4–5 minutes. (Cook in batches to stop them from sticking together.) Drain thoroughly. Serve topped with Bolognese sauce. Serve grated Parmesan cheese separately.

NUTRITIONAL NOTES

Per portion:

ENERGY 321 calories **FAT** 8.8g
SATURATED FAT 3g **CHOLESTEROL** 158mg
CARBOHYDRATE 32g **FIBER** 2g

Spaghetti alla Carbonara

Serves 4

INGREDIENTS

5 ounces smoked turkey bacon
1 medium onion, chopped
1–2 garlic cloves, crushed
²/₃ cup chicken stock
²/₃ cup dry white wine
7 ounces low-fat cream cheese
1 pound chili and garlic-
　flavored spaghetti
2 tablespoons chopped
　fresh parsley
salt and ground black pepper
shavings of Parmesan cheese,
　to serve

garlic

*flavored
spaghetti*

parsley

*smoked turkey
bacon*

*low-fat cream
cheese*

onion

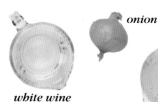

white wine

stock

1 Cut the turkey bacon into ¹/₂-inch strips. Fry quickly in a non-stick pan for 2–3 minutes. Add the onion, garlic and stock to the pan. Bring to a boil, cover and simmer for 5 minutes until tender.

2 Add the wine and boil rapidly until reduced by half. Whisk in the cream cheese until smooth.

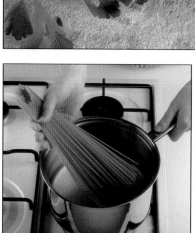

3 Meanwhile cook the spaghetti in a large pan of boiling, salted water for 10–12 minutes. Drain thoroughly.

4 Return to the pan with the sauce and parsley, toss well and serve immediately with shavings of Parmesan cheese.

NUTRITIONAL NOTES

PER PORTION:

ENERGY 500 calories **FAT** 3.3g
SATURATED FAT 0.5g **CHOLESTEROL** 21mg
CARBOHYDRATE 89g **FIBER** 4g

Pasta Shells with Tomato and Tuna Sauce

Serves 6

INGREDIENTS

1 medium onion, finely chopped
1 stick celery, finely chopped
1 red bell pepper, seeded and diced
1 garlic clove, crushed
$2/3$ cup chicken stock
14 ounce can chopped tomatoes
1 tablespoon tomato paste
2 teaspoons caster sugar
1 tablespoon chopped fresh basil
1 tablespoon chopped fresh parsley
1 pound dried pasta shells
14 ounce canned tuna packed in
    water, drained
2 tablespoons capers in
    vinegar, drained
salt and ground black pepper

celery

canned
tuna

tomato
paste

capers

garlic

bell pepper

stock

onion

chopped
tomatoes

basil

parsley

1 Put the chopped onion, celery, pepper and garlic into a non-stick pan. Add the stock, bring to a boil and cook for 5 minutes or until the stock is reduced almost completely.

2 Add the tomatoes, tomato paste, sugar and herbs. Season to taste and bring to a boil. Simmer for 30 minutes until thick, stirring occasionally.

3 Meanwhile cook the pasta in a large pan of boiling, salted water according to package instructions. Drain thoroughly and transfer to a warm serving dish.

4 Flake the tuna into large chunks and add to the sauce with the capers. Heat gently for 1–2 minutes, pour over the pasta, toss gently and serve at once.

NUTRITIONAL NOTES

PER PORTION:

ENERGY 369 calories **FAT** 2.1g
SATURATED FAT 0.4g **CHOLESTEROL** 34mg
CARBOHYDRATE 65g **FIBER** 4g

Tortellini

Serves 6–8 as a starter or 4–6 as a main course

INGREDIENTS
4 ounces smoked lean ham
4 ounces chicken breast, boned and
 skinned
3³/₄ cups chicken or vegetable stock
cilantro stalks
2 tablespoons grated Parmesan
 cheese, plus extra for serving
1 egg, beaten, plus egg white
 for brushing
2 tablespoons chopped
 fresh cilantro
1 recipe basic pasta dough
flour, for dusting
salt and ground black pepper
cilantro leaves, to garnish

basic pasta dough

smoked ham

chicken breast

grated Parmesan cheese

stock

cilantro

egg

1 Cut the ham and chicken into large chunks and put them into a saucepan with ²/₃ cup of the chicken or vegetable stock and some cilantro stalks. Bring to a boil, cover and simmer for 20 minutes until tender. Cool the stock slightly.

2 Drain the ham and chicken and mince finely (reserve the stock). Put into a bowl with the Parmesan cheese, beaten egg, chopped cilantro and season with salt and pepper.

3 Roll the pasta into thin sheets, cut into 1¹/₂-inch squares. Put ¹/₂ teaspoon of filling on each. Brush edges with egg white and fold each square into a triangle; press out any air and seal firmly.

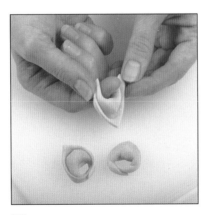

4 Curl each triangle around the tip of a forefinger and press the two ends together firmly.

5 Lay on a lightly floured tea towel to rest for 30 minutes before cooking.

NUTRITIONAL NOTES
PER PORTION:

ENERGY 335 calories **FAT** 9.7g
SATURATED FAT 3.6g **CHOLESTEROL** 193mg
CARBOHYDRATE 39g **FIBER** 1.6g

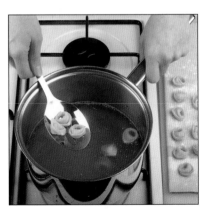

6 Strain the reserved stock and add to the remainder. Put into a pan and bring to a boil. Lower the heat to a gentle boil and add the tortellini. Cook for 5 minutes. Then turn off the heat, cover the pan and let stand for 20–30 minutes. Serve in soup plates with some of the stock and garnish with cilantro leaves. Serve grated Parmesan separately.

Penne with Salmon and Dill

Serves 6

INGREDIENTS

12 ounces fresh salmon
  fillet, skinned
4 ounces sliced smoked salmon
1–2 shallots, finely chopped
4 ounces button mushrooms,
  quartered
²/₃ cup light red or rosé wine
²/₃ cup fish stock
²/₃ cup low-fat sour cream
2 tablespoons chopped fresh dill
12 ounces penne
salt and ground black pepper
sprigs of dill, to garnish

1 Cut the fresh salmon into 1-inch cubes. Cut the smoked salmon into ¹/₂-inch strips.

2 Put the shallots and mushrooms into a non-stick pan with the red or rosé wine. Bring to a boil and cook for about 5 minutes or until the wine is reduced almost completely.

3 Add the fish stock and sour cream and stir until smooth. Then add the fresh salmon, cover the pan and cook gently for 2–3 minutes.

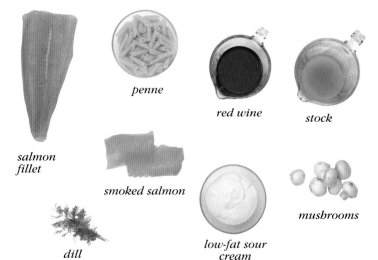

penne

red wine

stock

salmon fillet

smoked salmon

low-fat sour cream

mushrooms

dill

4 Remove from the heat and stir in the chopped dill and seasoning.

5 Meanwhile cook the pasta in a large pan of boiling, salted water according to the instructions on the package. Drain thoroughly and transfer to a warm serving dish. Add the smoked salmon to the sauce and pour over the pasta. Toss lightly to mix. Serve at once, garnished with sprigs of dill.

NUTRITIONAL NOTES

PER PORTION:

ENERGY 394 calories **FAT** 12.8g
SATURATED FAT 4.6g **CHOLESTEROL** 64mg
CARBOHYDRATE 45g **FIBER** 2g

Shrimp and Pasta Salad with Green Dressing

Serves 4–6

INGREDIENTS
4 anchovy fillets, drained
4 tablespoons skim milk
8 ounces squid
1 tablespoon chopped capers
1 tablespoon chopped cornichons
1–2 garlic cloves, crushed
²/₃ cup low-fat plain yogurt
2–3 tablespoons reduced-fat
    mayonnaise
squeeze of lemon juice
2 ounces watercress, finely chopped
2 tablespoons chopped fresh parsley
2 tablespoons chopped fresh basil
12 ounces fusilli
12 ounces peeled shrimp
salt and ground black pepper

squid   *anchovy fillets*

cornichons and capers

watercress

parsley

low-fat plain yogurt

shrimp

fusilli   *reduced-fat mayonnaise*

garlic *lemon*

basil

1 Put the anchovies into a small bowl and cover with the skim milk. Leave to soak for 10 minutes to remove the oil and strong salty flavor. Pull the head from the body of each squid and remove the quill. Peel outer speckled skin from the bodies. Cut the tentacles from the heads and rinse under cold water. Cut into ¼-inch rings.

2 To make the dressing, mix the capers, cornichons, garlic, yogurt, mayonnaise, lemon juice and fresh herbs in a bowl. Drain and chop the anchovies. Add to the dressing with the seasoning.

3 Drop the squid rings into a large pan of boiling, salted water. Lower the heat and simmer for 1–2 minutes. (Do not overcook or the squid will become tough.) Remove with a slotted spoon. Cook the pasta in the same water according to the instructions on the package. Drain thoroughly.

4 Mix the shrimp and squid into the dressing in a large bowl. Add the pasta, toss and serve warm or cold as a salad.

NUTRITIONAL NOTES

PER PORTION:

ENERGY 502 calories **FAT** 6.9g
SATURATED FAT 1.1g **CHOLESTEROL** 72mg
CARBOHYDRATE 71g **FIBER** 3.2g

Crab Pasta Salad with Spicy Cocktail Dressing

Serves 6

INGREDIENTS

12 ounces fusilli
1 small red bell pepper, seeded and
    finely chopped
2 x 6-ounce cans white crab
    meat, drained
4 ounces cherry tomatoes, halved
¼ cucumber, halved, seeded and
    sliced into crescents
1 tablespoon lemon juice
1¼ cups low-fat yogurt
2 sticks celery, finely chopped
2 teaspoons horseradish cream
½ teaspoon ground paprika
½ teaspoon Dijon mustard
2 tablespoons salsa
salt and ground black pepper
fresh basil, to garnish

celery

paprika

lemon

red pepper *fusilli*

cucumber

crab meat

cherry tomatoes

low-fat yogurt

salsa *horseradish cream*

1 Cook the pasta in a large pan of boiling, salted water according to the instructions on the package. Drain and rinse thoroughly under cold water.

2 Cover the chopped red bell pepper with boiling water and let stand for 1 minute. Drain and rinse under cold water. Pat dry with paper towels.

NUTRITIONAL NOTES

PER PORTION:

ENERGY 305 calories **FAT** 2.5g
SATURATED FAT 0.5g **CHOLESTEROL** 43mg
CARBOHYDRATE 53g **FIBER** 2.9g

3 Drain the crab meat and pick over carefully for pieces of shell. Put into a bowl with the halved tomatoes and sliced cucumber. Season with salt and pepper and sprinkle with lemon juice.

4 To make the dressing, add the red pepper to the yogurt, celery, horseradish, paprika, mustard and salsa. Mix the pasta with the dressing and transfer to a serving dish. Spoon the crab mixture on top and garnish with fresh basil.

Hot Spicy Shrimp with Campanelle

Serves 4–6

INGREDIENTS

8 ounces jumbo shrimp, cooked
    and peeled
1–2 garlic cloves, crushed
finely grated rind of 1 lemon
1 tablespoon lemon juice
¼ teaspoon red chili paste
1 tablespoon light soy sauce
5 ounces smoked turkey bacon
1 shallot or small onion,
    finely chopped
4 tablespoons white wine
8 ounces campanelle
4 tablespoons fish stock
4 firm ripe tomatoes, peeled, seeded
    and chopped
2 tablespoons chopped fresh parsley
salt and ground black pepper

campanelle

parsley

lemon

garlic

tomatoes

turkey bacon

stock

shrimp

onion

white wine

soy sauce

1 In a glass bowl, mix the shrimp with the garlic, lemon rind and juice, chili paste and soy sauce. Season with salt and pepper, cover and marinate the shrimp for at least 1 hour.

2 Grill the turkey bacon, then cut them into ¼-inch dice.

3 Put the shallot or onion and white wine into a pan, bring to the boil, cover and cook for 2–3 minutes or until tender and the wine is reduced by half.

4 Cook the campanelle in a large pan of boiling, salted water until *al dente*. Drain thoroughly.

5 Just before serving, put the shrimp with their marinade into a large frying pan, bring to the boil quickly and add the smoked turkey and fish stock. Heat through for 1 minute.

6 Add to the pasta with the chopped tomatoes and parsley, toss quickly and serve immediately.

NUTRITIONAL NOTES

PER PORTION:

ENERGY 331 calories **FAT** 2.9g
SATURATED FAT 0.6g **CHOLESTEROL** 64mg
CARBOHYDRATE 48g **FIBER** 3.2g

Smoked Haddock in Parsley Sauce

Serves 4

INGREDIENTS
1 pound smoked haddock fillet
1 small leek or onion, sliced thickly
1¼ cups skim milk
a bouquet garni (bay leaf, thyme
    and parsley)
1 ounce low-fat margarine
1 ounce flour
2 tablespoons chopped fresh parsley
8 ounces pasta shells
salt and ground black pepper
½ ounce toasted slivered almonds,
    to serve

haddock fillet

leek   *salt*

parsley

bay leaves

pepper

pasta shells

skim milk

flour

low-fat margarine

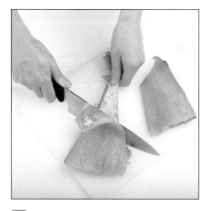

1 Remove all the skin and any bones from the haddock. Put into a pan with the leek or onion, milk and bouquet garni. Bring to a boil, cover and simmer gently for about 8–10 minutes until the fish flakes easily.

2 Strain, reserving the milk for making the sauce, and discard the bouquet garni.

NUTRITIONAL NOTES

PER PORTION:

ENERGY 405 calories **FAT** 6.9g
SATURATED FAT 1.0g **CHOLESTEROL** 42mg
CARBOHYDRATE 58g **FIBER** 3.7g

3 Put the margarine, flour and reserved milk into a pan. Bring to a boil and whisk until smooth. Season and add the fish and leek or onion.

4 Cook the pasta in a large pan of boiling water until *al dente*. Drain thoroughly and stir into the sauce with the chopped parsley. Serve immediately, scattered with almonds.

Fusilli with Smoked Trout

Serves 4–6

INGREDIENTS

2 carrots, cut in julienne sticks
1 leek, cut in julienne sticks
2 sticks celery, cut in julienne sticks
²/₃ cup vegetable stock
8 ounces fresh trout fillets, skinned and cut into strips
7 ounces low-fat cream cheese
²/₃ cup white wine or fish stock
1 tablespoon chopped fresh dill or fennel
8 ounces fusilli
salt and ground black pepper
dill sprigs, to garnish

leek
carrots
low-fat cream cheese
celery
dill
white wine
trout fillets
stock
fusilli

1 Put the carrots, leek and celery into a pan with the vegetable stock. Bring to the boil and cook quickly for 4–5 minutes until tender and most of the stock has evaporated. Remove from the heat and add the smoked trout.

2 To make the sauce, put the cream cheese and wine or fish stock into a saucepan, heat and whisk until smooth. Season with salt and pepper. Add the chopped dill or fennel.

3 Cook the fusilli in a large pan of boiling, salted water until *al dente*. Drain thoroughly.

4 Return the fusilli to the pan with the sauce, toss lightly and transfer to a serving bowl. Top with the cooked vegetables and trout. Serve immediately, garnished with dill sprigs.

NUTRITIONAL NOTES

PER PORTION:

ENERGY 339 calories **FAT** 4.7g
SATURATED FAT 0.8g **CHOLESTEROL** 57mg
CARBOHYDRATE 49g **FIBER** 4.1g

Saffron Pappardelle

Serves 4

INGREDIENTS

large pinch of saffron strands
4 sun-dried tomatoes, chopped
1 teaspoon fresh thyme
12 large shrimp in their shells
8 ounces baby squid
8 ounces monkfish fillet
2–3 garlic cloves, crushed
2 small onions, quartered
1 small bulb fennel, trimmed
    and sliced
²/₃ cup white wine
8 ounces pappardelle
salt and ground black pepper
2 tablespoons chopped fresh
    parsley, to garnish

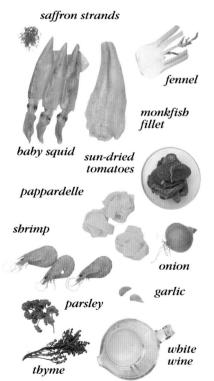

saffron strands

fennel

monkfish fillet

baby squid

sun-dried tomatoes

pappardelle

shrimp

onion

garlic

parsley

white wine

thyme

1 Put the saffron, sun-dried tomatoes and thyme into a bowl with 4 tablespoons hot water. Let soak for 30 minutes.

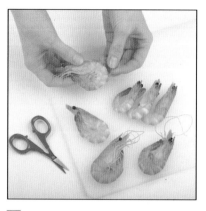

2 Wash the shrimp and carefully remove the shells, leaving the heads and tails intact. Pull the head from the body of each squid and remove the quill. Cut the tentacles from the head and rinse under cold water. Pull off the outer skin and cut into ¼-inch rings. Cut the monkfish into 1-inch cubes.

3 Put the garlic, onions and fennel into a pan with the wine. Cover and simmer for 5 minutes until tender.

4 Add the monkfish, saffron, tomatoes and thyme in their liquid. Cover and cook for 3 minutes. Then add the shrimp and squid. Cover and cook gently for 1–2 minutes. (Do not overcook or the squid will become tough.)

5 Meanwhile cook the pasta in a large pan of boiling, salted water until *al dente*. Drain thoroughly.

6 Divide the pasta among four serving dishes and top with the fish and shellfish sauce. Sprinkle with parsley and serve at once.

NUTRITIONAL NOTES

PER PORTION:

ENERGY 381 calories **FAT** 3.5g
SATURATED FAT 0.6g **CHOLESTEROL** 34mg
CARBOHYDRATE 52g **FIBER** 3.2g

Sweet and Sour Shrimp with Chinese Egg Noodles

Serves 4–6

INGREDIENTS

½ ounce dried porcini mushrooms
1¼ cups hot water
bunch of scallions, cut into thick
    diagonal slices
1-inch piece of fresh ginger, peeled
    and grated
1 red bell pepper, seeded and diced
8 ounce can water chestnuts, sliced
3 tablespoons light soy sauce
2 tablespoons sherry
12 ounces large peeled shrimp
8 ounces Chinese egg noodles

fresh ginger

red pepper

shrimp

scallions

water chestnuts

egg noodles

soy sauce

porcini mushrooms

1 Put the dried porcini mushrooms into a bowl with the hot water and soak for 15 minutes.

2 Put the scallions, ginger and diced red pepper into a pan with the mushrooms and their liquid. Bring to a boil, cover and cook for about 5 minutes until tender.

NUTRITIONAL NOTES

PER PORTION:

ENERGY 391 calories **FAT** 7.1g
SATURATED FAT 0.3g **CHOLESTEROL** 88mg
CARBOHYDRATE 54g **FIBER** 2.8g

3 Add the water chestnuts, soy sauce, sherry and shrimp. Cover and cook gently for 2 minutes.

4 Cook the egg noodles according to the instructions on the package. Drain thoroughly and transfer to a warmed serving dish. Spoon the hot shrimp on top. Serve at once.

Pasta with Scallops in Warm Green Tartare Sauce

Serves 4

INGREDIENTS
½ cup low-fat sour cream
2 teaspoons coarse-grained mustard
2 garlic cloves, crushed
2–3 tablespoons fresh lime juice
4 tablespoons chopped fresh parsley
2 tablespoons snipped chives
12 ounces black tagliatelle
12 large scallops
4 tablespoons white wine
⅔ cup fish stock
salt and ground black pepper
lime wedges and parsley sprigs,
    to garnish

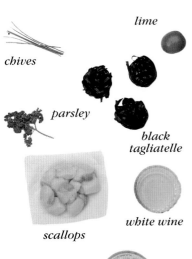

lime

chives

parsley

*black
tagliatelle*

scallops

white wine

*low-fat sour
cream*

fish stock

garlic

1 To make the tartare sauce, mix the sour cream, mustard, garlic, lime juice, herbs and seasoning together in a bowl.

2 Cook the pasta in a large pan of boiling, salted water until *al dente*. Drain thoroughly.

NUTRITIONAL NOTES

PER PORTION:

ENERGY 433 calories **FAT** 3.4g
SATURATED FAT 0.6g **CHOLESTEROL** 45mg
CARBOHYDRATE 68g **FIBER** 3.4g

3 Slice the scallops in half, horizontally. Put the white wine and fish stock into a saucepan. Heat to simmering point. Add the scallops and cook very gently for 3–4 minutes (no longer or they will become tough).

4 Remove the scallops. Boil the wine and stock to reduce by half and add the green sauce to the pan. Heat gently to warm, replace the scallops and cook for 1 minute. Spoon over the pasta and garnish with lime wedges and parsley.

Rolled Stuffed Cannelloni

Serves 4

INGREDIENTS
12 sheets lasagne
fresh basil leaves, to garnish

FOR THE FILLING
2–3 garlic cloves, crushed
1 small onion, finely chopped
²/₃ cup white wine
1 pound ground turkey
1 tablespoon dried basil
1 tablespoon dried thyme
1½ ounces fresh white bread
    crumbs

FOR THE SAUCE
1 ounce low-fat margarine
1 ounce flour
1¼ cups skim milk
4 sun-dried tomatoes, chopped
1 tablespoon chopped fresh herbs
    (basil, parsley, marjoram)
2 tablespoons grated
    Parmesan cheese
salt and ground black pepper

skim milk

sliced white bread

lasagne

sun-dried tomatoes

ground turkey

parsley

grated Parmesan cheese

white wine

onion

flour

low-fat margarine

basil

1 Put the garlic, onion and half the wine into a pan. Cover and cook for about 5 minutes until tender. Increase the heat, add the turkey and break up the pieces with a wooden spoon. Cook quickly until all the liquid has evaporated and the turkey begins to brown.

2 Lower the heat, add the remaining wine, seasoning and dried herbs. Cover and cook for 20 minutes. Remove from the heat and stir in the bread crumbs. Leave to cool.

3 Cook the lasagne sheets in a large pan of boiling, salted water until *al dente*. Cook in batches to prevent them from sticking together. Drain thoroughly and rinse in cold water. Pat dry on a clean dish towel.

4 Lay the lasagne on a chopping board. Spoon the turkey mixture along one short edge and roll it up to encase the filling. Cut the tubes in half.

5 Preheat the oven to 400°F. Put the margarine, flour and skim milk into a pan, heat and whisk until smooth. Add the chopped tomatoes, fresh herbs and seasoning.

6 Spoon a thin layer of the sauce into a shallow ovenproof dish and arrange a layer of cannelloni on top. Spoon over a layer of sauce and cover with more cannelloni and sauce. Sprinkle with grated Parmesan and bake for 10–15 minutes until lightly browned. Serve at once, garnished with fresh basil leaves.

NUTRITIONAL NOTES
PER PORTION:

ENERGY 336 calories **FAT** 7.4g
SATURATED FAT 2.7g **CHOLESTEROL** 65mg
CARBOHYDRATE 26g **FIBER** 1.4g

Chili Mince and Pipe Rigati

Serves 6

INGREDIENTS

1 pound extra lean ground beef
   or turkey
1 onion, finely chopped
2–3 garlic cloves, crushed
1–2 red chilies, seeded and
   finely chopped
14-ounce can chopped tomatoes
3 tablespoons tomato paste
1 teaspoon mixed dried herbs
1¾ cups water
1 pound pipe rigati
14-ounce can red kidney beans,
   drained
salt and ground black pepper

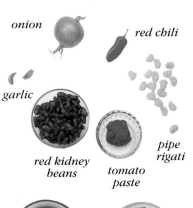

onion

red chili

garlic

red kidney beans

tomato paste

pipe rigati

chopped tomatoes

ground beef

1 Cook the ground beef or turkey in a non-stick saucepan, breaking up any large pieces with a wooden spoon until browned all over.

2 Add the onion, garlic and chilies, cover with a lid and cook gently for 5 minutes.

NUTRITIONAL NOTES

PER PORTION:

ENERGY 425 calories **FAT** 5.4g
SATURATED FAT 1.4g **CHOLESTEROL** 44mg
CARBOHYDRATE 70g **FIBER** 6.1g

3 Add the tomatoes, tomato paste, herbs, water and seasoning. Bring to a boil and simmer for 1½ hours. Leave to cool slightly.

4 Cook the pasta in a large pan of boiling, salted water until *al dente*. Drain thoroughly. Skim off any fat that rises to the surface. Add the red kidney beans and heat for 5–10 minutes. Pour over the cooked pasta, and serve.

Turkey and Pasta Casserole

Serves 4

INGREDIENTS

10 ounces ground turkey
5 ounces smoked turkey
    bacon, chopped
1–2 garlic cloves, crushed
1 onion, finely chopped
2 carrots, diced
2 tablespoons concentrated
    tomato paste
1¼ cups chicken stock
8 ounces rigatoni
2 tablespoons grated
    Parmesan cheese
salt and ground black pepper

turkey bacon *carrots* *onion*

rigatoni

garlic

tomato purée

Parmesan cheese

ground turkey   *stock*

1 Brown the ground turkey in a non-stick saucepan, breaking up any large pieces with a wooden spoon, until well browned all over.

2 Add the chopped turkey bacon, garlic, onion, carrots, paste, stock and seasoning. Bring to a boil, cover and simmer for 1 hour until tender.

3 Preheat the oven to 350°F. Cook the pasta in a large pan of boiling, salted water until *al dente*. Drain thoroughly and mix with the turkey sauce.

4 Transfer to a shallow ovenproof dish and sprinkle with grated Parmesan cheese. Bake in the preheated oven for 20–30 minutes until lightly browned.

NUTRITIONAL NOTES

PER PORTION:

ENERGY 391 calories **FAT** 4.9g
SATURATED FAT 2.2g **CHOLESTEROL** 60mg
CARBOHYDRATE 55g **FIBER** 3.5g

Ham-filled Paprika Ravioli

Serves 4

INGREDIENTS
8 ounces cooked smoked ham
4 tablespoons mango chutney
1 recipe basic pasta dough, with
    1 teaspoon ground paprika
    added
egg white, beaten
flour, for dusting
1–2 garlic cloves, crushed
1 stick celery, sliced
2 ounces sun-dried tomatoes
1 red chili, seeded and chopped
⅔ cup red wine
14-ounce can chopped tomatoes
1 teaspoons chopped fresh thyme,
    plus extra to garnish
2 teaspoons sugar
salt and ground black pepper

garlic

celery   *red chili*   *smoked ham*

thyme   *red wine*

sun-dried tomatoes   *chopped tomatoes*

mango chutney   *basic pasta dough*   *paprika*

1 Remove all traces of fat from the ham, place it with the mango chutney in a food processor or blender and mince the mixture finely.

2 Roll the pasta into thin sheets and lay one piece over a ravioli tray. Put a teaspoonful of the ham filling into each of the depressions.

3 Brush around the edges of each ravioli with egg white. Cover with another sheet of pasta and press the edges together to seal.

4 Using a rolling pin, roll over the top of the dough to cut and seal each pocket. Transfer to a floured dish towel and let rest for 1 hour before cooking.

5 Put the garlic, celery, sun-dried tomatoes, chili, wine, canned tomatoes and thyme into a pan. Cover and cook for 15–20 minutes. Season with salt, pepper and sugar.

6 Cook the ravioli in a large pan of boiling, salted water for 4–5 minutes. Drain thoroughly. Spoon a little of the sauce onto a serving plate and arrange the ravioli on top. Sprinkle with fresh thyme and serve at once.

NUTRITIONAL NOTES
PER PORTION:

ENERGY 380 calories **FAT** 7.6g
SATURATED FAT 2.1g **CHOLESTEROL** 152mg
CARBOHYDRATE 52g **FIBER** 2.4g

Deviled Ham and Pineapple Salad

Serves 4

INGREDIENTS
8 ounces whole wheat penne
²/₃ cup low-fat yogurt
1 tablespoon cider vinegar
1 teaspoon wholegrain mustard
large pinch of sugar
2 tablespoons hot mango chutney
4 ounces cooked lean ham, cubed
7 ounce can pineapple chunks
2 sticks celery, chopped
½ green bell pepper, seeded
    and diced
1 tablespoon toasted slivered
    almonds, chopped roughly
salt and ground black pepper
crusty bread, to serve

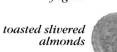
celery

green pepper

whole wheat penne

hot mango chutney

pineapple chunks *low-fat yogurt* *lean ham*

toasted slivered almonds

1 Cook the pasta in a large pan of boiling, salted water until *al dente*. Drain and rinse thoroughly. Let cool.

2 To make the dressing, mix the yogurt, vinegar, mustard, sugar and mango chutney together. Season, add the pasta and toss lightly together.

3 Transfer the pasta to a serving dish. Top with the ham, pineapple, celery and pepper.

4 Sprinkle with toasted almonds. Serve with crusty bread.

NUTRITIONAL NOTES
PER PORTION:

ENERGY 303 calories **FAT** 5.4g
SATURATED FAT 0.9g **CHOLESTEROL** 18.5mg
CARBOHYDRATE 51g **FIBER** 6g

Curried Chicken Salad

Serves 4

INGREDIENTS

2 cooked chicken breasts, boned
6 ounces green beans
12 ounces multi-colored penne
²/₃ cup low-fat yogurt
1 teaspoon mild curry powder
1 garlic clove, crushed
1 green chili, seeded and
    finely chopped
2 tablespoons chopped
    fresh cilantro
4 firm ripe tomatoes, peeled, seeded
    and cut in strips
salt and ground black pepper
fresh cilantro leaves, to garnish

*multi-colored
penne*

*chicken
breasts*

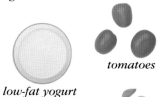

green chili

cilantro

green beans

tomatoes

low-fat yogurt

garlic

1 Remove the skin from the chicken and cut in strips. Cut the green beans in 1-inch lengths and cook in boiling water for 5 minutes. Drain and rinse under cold water.

2 Cook the pasta in a large pan of boiling, salted water until *al dente*. Drain and rinse thoroughly.

3 To make the sauce, mix the yogurt, curry powder, garlic, chilli and chopped cilantro together in a bowl. Stir in the chicken pieces and let stand for 30 minutes.

4 Transfer the pasta to a glass bowl and toss with the beans and tomatoes. Spoon over the chicken and sauce. Garnish with cilantro leaves.

NUTRITIONAL NOTES

PER PORTION:

ENERGY 449 calories **FAT** 5.1g
SATURATED FAT 1.3g **CHOLESTEROL** 38mg
CARBOHYDRATE 74g **FIBER** 4.9g

Duck Breast Salad

Serves 6

INGREDIENTS
2 duck breasts, boned
1 teaspoon coriander seeds, crushed
12 ounces rigatoni
²/₃ cup fresh orange juice
1 tablespoon lemon juice
2 teaspoons honey
1 shallot, finely chopped
1 garlic clove, crushed
1 stalk celery, chopped
3 ounces dried cherries
3 tablespoons port
1 tablespoon chopped fresh mint,
    plus extra for garnish
2 tablespoons chopped fresh
    cilantro, plus extra for garnish
1 apple, diced
2 oranges, segmented
salt and ground black pepper

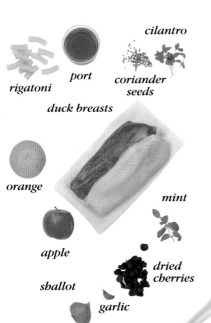

rigatoni   port   cilantro
                  coriander
                  seeds
duck breasts

orange
mint

apple
            dried
            cherries
shallot
    garlic

celery

1 Remove the skin and fat from the duck breasts and season with salt and pepper. Rub with crushed coriander seeds. Cook under a preheated broiler for 7–10 minutes depending on size. Wrap in foil and leave for 20 minutes.

2 Cook the pasta in a large pan of boiling, salted water until *al dente*. Drain thoroughly and rinse under cold running water. Let to cool.

3 To make the dressing, put the orange juice, lemon juice, honey, shallot, garlic, celery, cherries, port, mint and fresh cilantro into a bowl, whisk together and leave to marinate for 30 minutes.

4 Slice the duck very thinly. (It should be pink in the center.)

5 Put the pasta into a bowl, add the dressing, diced apple and segments of orange. Toss well to coat the pasta. Transfer the salad to a serving plate with the duck slices and garnish with the extra coriander and mint.

NUTRITIONAL NOTES
PER PORTION:

ENERGY 348 calories **FAT** 3.8g
SATURATED FAT 0.9g **CHOLESTEROL** 55mg
CARBOHYDRATE 64g **FIBER** 1.3g

Herbed Beef Salad

Serves 6

INGREDIENTS
1 pound beef fillet
1 pound fresh tagliatelle with
    sun-dried tomatoes and herbs
4 ounces cherry tomatoes
½ cucumber

FOR THE MARINADE
1 tablespoon soy sauce
1 tablespoon sherry
1 tablespoon fresh ginger, grated
1 garlic clove, crushed

FOR THE HERB DRESSING
2–3 tablespoons horseradish
⅔ cup low-fat yogurt
1 garlic clove, crushed
2–3 tablespoons chopped fresh
    herbs (chives, parsley, thyme)
salt and ground black pepper

cherry
tomatoes

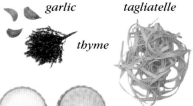

cucumber

fillet beef

fresh ginger

garlic

tagliatelle

thyme

low-fat
yogurt

horseradish
sauce

parsley

soy sauce

chives

1 Mix all the marinade ingredients together in a shallow dish, put the beef in and turn it over to coat it. Cover with plastic wrap and leave for 30 minutes to allow the flavors to penetrate the meat.

2 Preheat the grill. Lift the fillet out of the marinade and pat it dry with paper towels. Place on a broiler rack and broil for 8 minutes on each side, basting with the marinade during cooking.

3 Transfer to a plate, cover with foil and leave to stand for 20 minutes.

4 Put all the dressing ingredients into a bowl and mix together thoroughly. Cook the pasta according to the directions on the package, drain thoroughly, rinse under cold water and leave to dry.

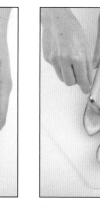

5 Cut the cherry tomatoes in half. Cut the cucumber in half lengthways, scoop out the seeds with a teaspoon and slice thinly into crescents.

6 Put the pasta, cherry tomatoes, cucumber and dressing into a bowl and toss to coat. Slice the beef thinly and arrange on a plate with the pasta salad.

NUTRITIONAL NOTES
PER PORTION:

ENERGY 374 calories **FAT** 5.7g
SATURATED FAT 1.7g **CHOLESTEROL** 46mg
CARBOHYDRATE 57g **FIBER** 2.9g

Pasta Primavera

Serves 4

INGREDIENTS
8 ounces thin asparagus spears, cut
　in half
4 ounces snow peas, trimmed
4 ounces whole baby corn
8 ounces whole baby
　carrots, trimmed
1 small red bell pepper, seeded
　and chopped
8 scallions, sliced
8 ounces torchietti or rotini
²/₃ cup low-fat cottage cheese
²/₃ cup low-fat yogurt
1 tablespoon lemon juice
1 tablespoon chopped parsley
1 tablespoon snipped chives
skim milk (optional)
salt and ground black pepper
sun-dried tomato bread, to serve

scallions　*baby corn*　*parsley*　*red pepper*

baby carrots　*lemon*

chives　*torchietti*

snow peas

asparagus spears

1 Cook the asparagus spears in a pan of boiling, salted water for 3–4 minutes. Add the snow peas halfway through the cooking time. Drain and rinse both under cold water.

2 Cook the baby corn, carrots, red pepper and spring onions in the same way until tender. Drain and rinse.

low-fat yogurt　*low-fat cottage cheese*

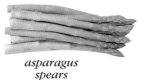

3 Cook the pasta in a large pan of boiling, salted water until *al dente*. Drain thoroughly.

NUTRITIONAL NOTES
PER PORTION:

ENERGY 320 calories **FAT** 3.1g
SATURATED FAT 0.4g **CHOLESTEROL** 3mg
CARBOHYDRATE 58g **FIBER** 6.2g

4 Put the cottage cheese, yogurt, lemon juice, parsley, chives and seasoning into a food processor or blender and process until smooth. Thin the sauce with skim milk, if necessary. Put into a large pan with the pasta and vegetables, heat gently and toss carefully. Transfer to a serving plate and serve with sun-dried tomato bread.

Tagliatelle with Mushrooms

Serves 4

INGREDIENTS
1 small onion, finely chopped
2 garlic cloves, crushed
$\frac{2}{3}$ cup vegetable stock
8 ounces mixed fresh mushrooms, such as button, oyster, or chanterelles
4 tablespoons white or red wine
2 teaspoons tomato paste
1 tablespoon soy sauce
1 teaspoon chopped fresh thyme
2 tablespoons chopped fresh parsley
8 ounces fresh sun-dried tomato and herb tagliatelle
salt and ground black pepper
shavings of Parmesan cheese, to serve (optional)

tomato paste

Parmesan cheese

onion

mixed mushrooms

thyme   *parsley*

vegetable stock

garlic

white wine

tagliatelle

soy sauce

1 Put the onion and garlic into a pan with the stock. Then cover and cook for 5 minutes or until tender.

2 Add the mushrooms (quartered or sliced if large or left whole if small), wine, tomato paste and soy sauce. Cover and cook for 5 minutes.

NUTRITIONAL NOTES
PER PORTION:

ENERGY 241 calories **FAT** 2.4g
SATURATED FAT 0.7g **CHOLESTEROL** 3mg
CARBOHYDRATE 45g **FIBER** 3g

3 Remove the lid from the pan and boil until the liquid is reduced by half. Stir in the chopped fresh herbs and season to taste.

4 Cook the pasta in a large pan of boiling, salted water until *al dente*. Drain thoroughly and toss lightly with the mushrooms. Serve at once with shavings of Parmesan cheese, if using.

Vegetarian Lasagne

Serves 6–8

INGREDIENTS

1 small eggplant
1 large onion, finely chopped
2 garlic cloves, crushed
²⁄₃ cup vegetable stock
8 ounces mushrooms, sliced
14 ounce can chopped tomatoes
2 tablespoons tomato paste
²⁄₃ cup red wine
¹⁄₄ teaspoon ground ginger
1 teaspoon mixed dried herbs
10–12 sheets lasagne
1 ounce low-fat margarine
1 ounce flour
1¹⁄₄ cups skim milk
large pinch of grated nutmeg
7 ounces low-fat cottage cheese
1 egg, beaten
¹⁄₂ ounce grated Parmesan cheese
1 ounce reduced-fat Cheddar
    cheese, grated
salt and ground black pepper

1 Wash the eggplant and cut it into 1-inch cubes. Put the onion and garlic into a saucepan with the stock, cover and cook for about 5 minutes or until tender.

2 Add the diced eggplant, sliced mushrooms, tomatoes, tomato paste, wine, ginger, seasoning and herbs. Bring to a boil, cover and cook for 15–20 minutes. Remove the lid and cook rapidly to reduce the liquid by half.

3 To make the sauce, put the margarine, flour, skim milk and nutmeg into a pan. Whisk together over the heat until thickened and smooth. Season to taste.

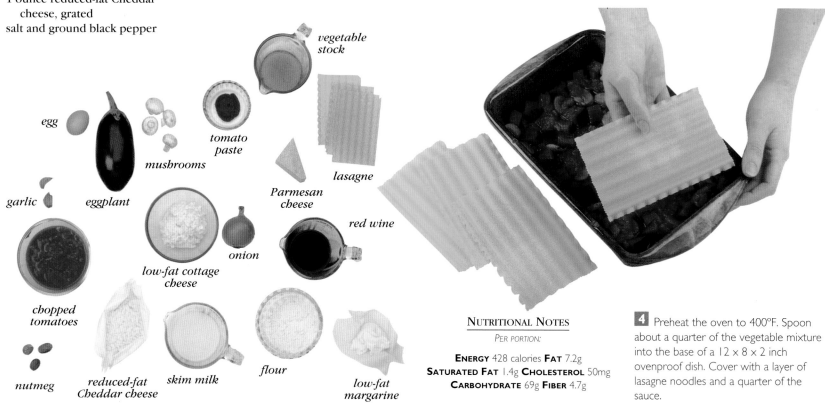

vegetable stock

egg

tomato paste

mushrooms

lasagne

garlic

eggplant

Parmesan cheese

red wine

onion

low-fat cottage cheese

chopped tomatoes

nutmeg

reduced-fat Cheddar cheese

skim milk

flour

low-fat margarine

NUTRITIONAL NOTES

PER PORTION:

ENERGY 428 calories **FAT** 7.2g
SATURATED FAT 1.4g **CHOLESTEROL** 50mg
CARBOHYDRATE 69g **FIBER** 4.7g

4 Preheat the oven to 400°F. Spoon about a quarter of the vegetable mixture into the base of a 12 x 8 x 2 inch ovenproof dish. Cover with a layer of lasagne noodles and a quarter of the sauce.

5 Repeat with two more layers, then cover with the cottage cheese. Beat the egg into the remaining sauce and pour over the top. Sprinkle with the two grated cheeses.

6 Bake for 25–30 minutes or until the top is golden brown.

Crescent Spinach Ravioli

Serves 4–6

INGREDIENTS
1 bunch of scallions, finely chopped
1 carrot, coarsely grated
2 garlic cloves, crushed
7 ounces low-fat cottage cheese
1 tablespoon chopped dill
4 halves sun-dried tomatoes,
    finely chopped
1 ounce grated Parmesan cheese
1 recipe basic pasta dough, with
    4 ounces frozen spinach, thawed
    and chopped added
egg white, beaten, for brushing
flour, for dusting
salt and ground black pepper
2 halves sun-dried tomatoes, finely
    chopped, and fresh dill,
    to garnish

carrot

sun-dried tomatoes

dill

garlic

scallions

Parmesan cheese

spinach

low-fat cottage cheese

1 Put the scallions, carrot, garlic and cottage cheese into a bowl. Add the chopped dill, tomatoes, seasoning and Parmesan cheese.

2 Roll the spinach pasta into thin sheets, cut into 3-inch rounds with a fluted pastry cutter.

3 Place a small spoonful of filling in the center of each circle. Brush the edges with egg white.

4 Fold each in half to make crescents. Press the edges together to seal. Transfer to a floured dish towel to let rest for 1 hour before cooking.

5 Cook the pasta in a large pan of boiling, salted water for 5 minutes. (Cook in batches to stop them sticking together.) Drain well.

6 Serve the crescents on warmed serving plates and garnish with sun-dried tomatoes and dill.

Nutritional Notes
Per Portion:

Energy 312 calories **Fat** 7.3g
Saturated Fat 2.4g **Cholesterol** 119mg
Carbohydrate 43g **Fiber** 3.4g

Vegetarian Cannelloni

Serves 4–6

INGREDIENTS

1 onion, finely chopped
2 garlic cloves, crushed
2 carrots, coarsely grated
2 stalks celery, finely chopped
$2/3$ cup vegetable stock
4 ounces red or green lentils
14 ounce can chopped tomatoes
2 tablespoons tomato purée
$1/2$ teaspoon ground ginger
1 teaspoon fresh thyme
1 teaspoon chopped fresh rosemary
$1^{1}/_{2}$ ounces low-fat margarine
$1^{1}/_{2}$ ounces flour
$2^{1}/_{2}$ cups skim milk
1 bay leaf
large pinch grated nutmeg
16–18 cannelloni tubes
1 ounce reduced-fat Cheddar
   cheese, grated
1 ounce grated Parmesan cheese
1 ounce fresh white bread crumbs
salt and ground black pepper
flat-leaf parsley, to garnish

1 To make the filling, put the onion, garlic, carrots and celery into a large saucepan. Add half the stock, cover and cook for 5 minutes or until tender.

2 Add the lentils, chopped tomatoes, tomato purée, ginger, thyme, rosemary and seasoning. Bring to a boil, cover and cook for 20 minutes. Remove the lid and cook for about 10 minutes until thick and soft. Let cool.

3 To make the sauce, put the margarine, flour, skim milk and bay leaf into a pan and whisk over the heat until thick and smooth. Season with salt, pepper and nutmeg. Discard the bay leaf.

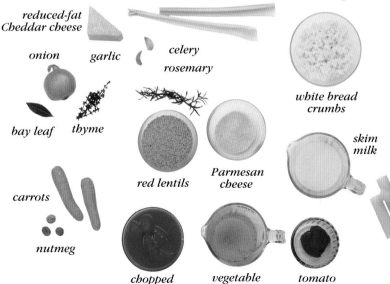

flour

low-fat margarine

reduced-fat Cheddar cheese

onion *garlic* *celery* *rosemary*

white bread crumbs

bay leaf *thyme*

skim milk

carrots

red lentils *Parmesan cheese*

nutmeg

chopped tomatoes *vegetable stock* *tomato purée*

cannelloni tubes

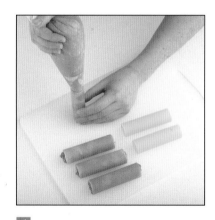

4 Fill the uncooked cannelloni by piping the filling into each tube. (It is easiest to hold them upright with one end flat on a cutting board, while piping into the other end.)

5 Preheat the oven to 350°F. Spoon half the sauce into the bottom of an 8-inch square ovenproof dish. Lay two rows of filled cannelloni on top and spoon over the remaining sauce.

6 Top with the cheeses and bread crumbs. Bake in the preheated oven for 30–40 minutes. Place under broiler to brown the top, if necessary. Garnish with flat-leaf parsley.

NUTRITIONAL NOTES
PER PORTION:

ENERGY 579 calories **FAT** 9.8g
SATURATED FAT 2.7g **CHOLESTEROL** 13mg
CARBOHYDRATE 100g **FIBER** 5.7g

Tagliatelle with Spinach Gnocchi

Serves 4–6

INGREDIENTS
1 pound mixed flavored tagliatelle
flour, for dusting
shavings of Parmesan cheese,
    to garnish

FOR THE SPINACH GNOCCHI
1 pound frozen chopped spinach
1 small onion, finely chopped
1 garlic clove, crushed
1/4 teaspoon ground nutmeg
14 ounces low-fat cottage cheese
4 ounces dried white bread crumbs
3 ounces semolina or flour
2 ounces grated Parmesan cheese
3 egg whites
salt and pepper

FOR THE TOMATO SAUCE
1 onion, finely chopped
1 stick celery, finely chopped
1 red pepper, seeded and diced
1 garlic clove, crushed
2/3 cup vegetable stock
14 ounce can tomatoes
1 tablespoon tomato paste
2 teaspoons sugar
1 teaspoon dried oregano

1 To make the tomato sauce, put the chopped onion, celery, pepper and garlic into a non-stick pan. Add the stock, bring to a boil and cook for 5 minutes or until tender.

2 Add the tomatoes, tomato paste, sugar and oregano. Season to taste, bring to a boil and simmer for 30 minutes until thick, stirring occasionally.

3 Meanwhile, put the frozen spinach, onion and garlic into a saucepan, cover and cook until the spinach is defrosted. Remove the lid and increase the heat to remove excess water. Season with salt, pepper and nutmeg. Cool the spinach in a bowl, add the remaining ingredients and mix thoroughly.

celery

garlic

egg   *nutmeg*

onion

low-fat cottage cheese

flavored tagliatelle   *red pepper*

grated Parmesan cheese   *spinach*

dried white bread crumbs

vegetable stock

tomato paste   *tomatoes*   *semolina*

4 Shape the mixture into about 24 ovals with two dessertspoons and place them on a lightly floured tray. Place in the fridge for 30 minutes.

78

5 Have a large shallow pan of boiling, salted water ready. Cook the gnocchi in batches, for about 5 minutes. (The water should simmer gently and not boil.) As soon as the gnocchi rise to the surface, remove them with a slotted spoon and drain thoroughly.

6 Cook the tagliatelle in a large pan of boiling, salted water until *al dente*. Drain thoroughly. Transfer to warmed serving plates, top with gnocchi and spoon over the tomato sauce. Top with shavings of Parmesan cheese and serve at once.

NUTRITIONAL NOTES
PER PORTION:

ENERGY 789 calories **FAT** 10.9g
SATURATED FAT 3.7g **CHOLESTEROL** 20mg
CARBOHYDRATE 135g **FIBER** 8.1g

Tofu Stir-fry with Egg Noodles

Serves 4

INGREDIENTS

8 ounces firm tofu
3 tablespoons dark soy sauce
2 tablespoons sherry or vermouth
3 leeks, sliced thinly
1-inch piece fresh ginger, peeled
   and finely grated
1–2 red chilies, seeded and sliced in
   rings
1 small red bell pepper, seeded and
   sliced thinly
2/3 cup vegetable stock
2 teaspoons honey
2 teaspoons cornstarch
8 ounces medium egg noodles
salt and ground black pepper

leeks

egg
noodles

fresh
ginger

tofu

red
chilies

red bell
pepper

soy sauce

vegetable
stock

vermouth

1 Cut the tofu into ³/₄-inch cubes. Put it into a bowl with the soy sauce and the sherry or vermouth. Toss to coat each piece and marinate for about 30 minutes.

2 Put the leeks, ginger, chili, pepper and stock into a frying pan. Bring to a boil and cook quickly for 2–3 minutes until just soft.

3 Strain the tofu, reserving the marinade. Mix the honey and cornstarch into the marinade.

4 Put the egg noodles into a large pan of boiling water and let stand for about 6 minutes until cooked (or follow the instructions on the package).

5 Heat a non-stick frying pan and quickly fry the tofu until lightly golden brown on all sides.

6 In a saucepan, add the vegetable mixture to the tofu with the marinade, and stir well until the liquid is thick and glossy. Spoon onto the egg noodles and serve at once.

NUTRITIONAL NOTES

PER PORTION:

ENERGY 345 calories **FAT** 8.2g
SATURATED FAT 0.7g **CHOLESTEROL** 0mg
CARBOHYDRATE 55g **FIBER** 2.5g

Spicy Ratatouille and Penne

Serves 6

INGREDIENTS
1 small eggplant
2 zucchini, thickly sliced
7 ounces firm tofu, cubed
3 tablespoons dark soy sauce
1 garlic clove, crushed
2 teaspoons sesame seeds
1 small red bell pepper, seeded
    and sliced
1 onion, finely chopped
1–2 garlic cloves, crushed
²/₃ cup vegetable stock
3 firm ripe tomatoes, peeled, seeded
    and quartered
1 tablespoon chopped mixed herbs
8 ounces penne
salt and ground black pepper
crusty bread, to serve

tomatoes

zucchini

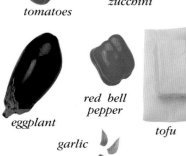

red bell
pepper

eggplant

tofu

garlic

onion

penne

sesame
seeds

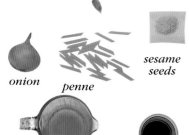

vegetable stock

soy sauce

1 Wash and cut the eggplant into 1-inch cubes. Put into a colander with the zucchini, sprinkle with salt and leave to drain for 30 minutes.

2 Mix the tofu with the soy sauce, garlic and sesame seeds. Cover and marinate for 30 minutes.

NUTRITIONAL NOTES

PER PORTION:

ENERGY 208 calories **FAT** 3.7g
SATURATED FAT 0.5g **CHOLESTEROL** 0mg
CARBOHYDRATE 36g **FIBER** 3.9g

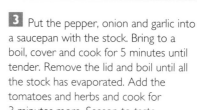

3 Put the pepper, onion and garlic into a saucepan with the stock. Bring to a boil, cover and cook for 5 minutes until tender. Remove the lid and boil until all the stock has evaporated. Add the tomatoes and herbs and cook for 3 minutes more. Season to taste.

4 Meanwhile cook the pasta in a large pan of boiling, salted water until *al dente*. Drain thoroughly. Toss the pasta with the vegetables and tofu. Transfer to a shallow 10-inch square ovenproof dish and grill until lightly browned. Transfer to a serving dish and serve with fresh crusty bread.

Mixed Bean Chili

Serves 6

INGREDIENTS

1 onion, finely chopped
1–2 garlic cloves, crushed
1 large green chili, seeded
  and chopped
²/₃ cup vegetable stock
14 ounce can chopped tomatoes
2 tablespoons tomato paste
½ cup red wine
1 teaspoon dried oregano
7 ounces green beans, sliced
14 ounce can red kidney
  beans, drained
14 ounce can cannellini
  beans, drained
14 ounce can chick-peas, drained
1 pound spaghetti
salt and ground black pepper

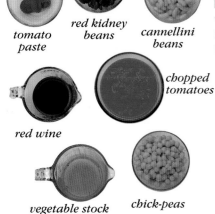

spaghetti

onion

green chili

garlic

green beans

tomato paste

red kidney beans

cannellini beans

red wine

chopped tomatoes

vegetable stock

chick-peas

1 To make the sauce, put the chopped onion, garlic and chili into a non-stick pan with the stock. Bring to a boil and cook for 5 minutes until tender.

2 Add the tomatoes, tomato paste, wine, seasoning and oregano. Bring to a boil, cover and simmer the sauce for 20 minutes.

NUTRITIONAL NOTES

PER PORTION:

ENERGY 431 calories **FAT** 3.6g
SATURATED FAT 0.2g **CHOLESTEROL** 0mg
CARBOHYDRATE 82g **FIBER** 9.9g

3 Cook the green beans in boiling, salted water for about 5–6 minutes until tender. Drain thoroughly.

4 Add all the beans to the sauce and simmer for 10 more minutes. Cook the spaghetti in a large pan of boiling, salted water until *al dente*. Drain thoroughly. Transfer to a serving dish and top with the chili beans.

Tex-Mex Chicken Salad

Serves 6

Ingredients

1 teaspoon ground cumin seeds
1 teaspoon ground paprika
1 teaspoon ground turmeric
1–2 garlic cloves, crushed
2 tablespoons lime juice
4 chicken breasts, boned
    and skinned
8 ounces rigatoni
1 red bell pepper, chopped
2 stalks celery, sliced thinly
1 shallot or small onion,
    finely chopped
1 ounce stuffed green
    olives, halved
2 tablespoons honey
1 tablespoon coarse-grained mustard
1–2 tablespoons lime juice
salt and ground black pepper
mixed salad, to serve

chicken breasts   *honey*

cumin seeds

red bell pepper   *onion*   *lime*

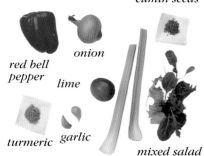

turmeric   *garlic*   *mixed salad*

celery

rigatoni   *stuffed olives*   *paprika*

1 Mix the cumin, paprika, turmeric, garlic, seasoning and lime juice in a bowl. Rub this mixture over the chicken breasts. Lay in a shallow dish, cover with plastic wrap and refrigerate for about 3 hours or overnight.

2 Preheat the oven to 400°F. Put the chicken in an ovenproof dish in a single layer and bake for 20 minutes (or broil for 8–10 minutes on each side).

3 Cook the rigatoni in a large pan of boiling, salted water until *al dente*. Drain and rinse under cold water. Pat dry with paper towels.

4 Put the red pepper, celery, shallot or small onion and olives into a large bowl with the pasta.

5 Mix the honey, mustard and lime juice together in a bowl and pour over the pasta. Toss to coat.

6 Cut the chicken in bite-size pieces. Arrange the mixed salad leaves on a serving dish, spoon the pasta mixture in the center and top with the spicy chicken pieces.

Nutritional Notes

Per portion

Energy 277 calories **Fat** 5.6g
Saturated Fat 1.4g **Cholesterol** 49mg
Carbohydrate 36g **Fiber** 2.1g

Piquant Chicken with Spaghetti

Serves 4

INGREDIENTS
1 onion, finely chopped
1 carrot, diced
1 garlic clove, crushed
1¼ cups vegetable stock or water
4 small chicken breasts, boned and skinned
bouquet garni (bay leaf, parsley and thyme)
4 ounces button mushrooms, sliced thinly
1 teaspoon wine vinegar or lemon juice
12 ounces spaghetti
½ cucumber, peeled and sliced lengthwise
2 firm ripe tomatoes, peeled, seeded and chopped
2 tablespoons low-fat sour cream
1 tablespoon chopped fresh parsley
1 tablespoon snipped chives
salt and ground black pepper

carrot

chicken breasts   *tomatoes*

cucumber
chives

thyme   *spaghetti*
parsley

button mushrooms   *bay leaf*

vegetable stock   *onion*

1 Put the onion, carrot, garlic, stock or water into a saucepan with the chicken breasts and bouquet garni. Bring to a boil, cover and simmer gently for 15–20 minutes or until tender. Transfer the chicken to a plate and cover with foil.

2 Remove the chicken and strain the liquid. Discard the vegetables and return the liquid to the pan. Add the sliced mushrooms, wine vinegar or lemon juice and simmer for 2–3 minutes until tender.

3 Cook the spaghetti in a large pan of boiling, salted water until *al dente*. Drain thoroughly.

4 Blanch the cucumber in boiling water for 10 seconds. Drain and rinse under cold water.

5 Cut the chicken breasts into bite-size pieces. Boil the stock to reduce by half, then add the chicken, tomatoes, sour cream, cucumber and herbs. Season with salt and pepper to taste.

6 Transfer the spaghetti to a warmed serving dish and spoon over the piquant chicken. Serve at once.

NUTRITIONAL NOTES
PER PORTION:

ENERGY 472 calories **FAT** 7.6g
SATURATED FAT 2.5g **CHOLESTEROL** 65mg
CARBOHYDRATE 72g **FIBER** 4.8g

Pappardelle and Provençal Sauce

Serves 4

INGREDIENTS
2 small purple onions, peeled
²/₃ cup vegetable stock
1–2 garlic cloves, crushed
4 tablespoons red wine
2 zucchini, sliced lengthwise
1 yellow bell pepper, seeded
    and sliced
14 ounce can tomatoes
2 teaspoons fresh thyme
1 teaspoon sugar
12 ounces pappardelle
salt and ground black pepper
fresh thyme and 6 black olives,
    stoned and coarsely chopped,
    to garnish

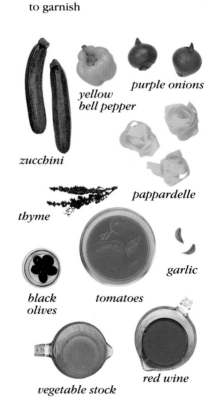

zucchini

yellow bell pepper

purple onions

thyme

pappardelle

garlic

black olives

tomatoes

vegetable stock

red wine

1 Cut each onion into eight wedges through the root end, so that they hold together during cooking. Put into a saucepan with the stock and garlic. Bring to the boil, cover and simmer for 5 minutes until tender.

2 Add the red wine, zucchini, yellow pepper, tomatoes, thyme, sugar and seasoning. Bring to a boil and cook gently for 5–7 minutes, shaking the pan occasionally to coat the vegetables with the sauce. (Do not overcook the vegetables, as they are much nicer if they are slightly crunchy.)

3 Cook the pasta in a large pan of boiling, salted water until *al dente*. Drain thoroughly.

4 Transfer the pasta to a warmed serving dish and top with the vegetables. Garnish with fresh thyme and chopped black olives.

NUTRITIONAL NOTES

PER PORTION:

ENERGY 369 calories **FAT** 2.5g
SATURATED FAT 0.4g **CHOLESTEROL** 0mg
CARBOHYDRATE 75g **FIBER** 4.3g

Fettuccine with Broccoli and Garlic

Serves 4

INGREDIENTS
3–4 garlic cloves, crushed
12 ounces broccoli florets
²/₃ cup chicken stock
4 tablespoons white wine
2 tablespoons chopped fresh basil
4 tablespoons grated
    Parmesan cheese
12 ounces fettuccine or tagliatelle
salt and pepper
fresh basil leaves, to garnish

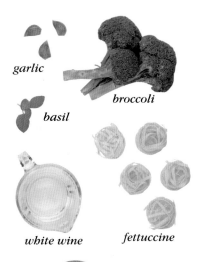

garlic

broccoli

basil

white wine   *fettuccine*

chicken stock   *grated Parmesan cheese*

1 Put the garlic, broccoli and stock into a saucepan. Bring to a boil and cook for 5 minutes until tender, stirring from time to time.

2 Mash with a fork or potato masher, until roughly chopped. Return to the pan with the white wine, basil and Parmesan cheese. Season to taste.

NUTRITIONAL NOTES
PER PORTION:

ENERGY 477 calories **FAT** 8.3g
SATURATED FAT 3.4g **CHOLESTEROL** 15mg
CARBOHYDRATE 71g **FIBER** 5g

3 Cook the fettuccine in a large pan of boiling, salted water until *al dente*. Drain thoroughly.

4 Return to the pan with half the broccoli sauce, toss to coat the pasta and transfer to serving plates. Top with the remaining broccoli sauce and garnish with basil leaves.

Deviled Crab Conchiglioni

Serves 4

INGREDIENTS
12 ounces pasta shells
7 ounces low-fat cream cheese
²/₃ cup skim milk
¹/₂ teaspoon ground paprika
1 teaspoon Dijon mustard
1 tablespoon dried bread crumbs
2 teaspoons grated Parmesan cheese
salt and pepper

FILLING
1 shallot, finely chopped
1 stick celery, finely chopped
¹/₂ small red bell pepper, seeded and
    finely chopped
3 tablespoons white wine
3 tablespoons low-fat sour cream
2 x 6 ounce cans crab meat in brine,
    drained
3 tablespoons fresh white bread
    crumbs
2 tablespoons grated
    Parmesan cheese
1 tablespoon Dijon mustard
¹/₂ teaspoon red chili paste

shallot

celery

pasta shells

white bread crumbs

red pepper

low-fat cream cheese

grated Parmesan cheese

low-fat sour cream

dried bread crumbs

crab meat

paprika

skim milk

white wine

1 Put the chopped shallot, celery and red pepper into a small pan with the white wine, cover and cook gently for 3–4 minutes until tender and the wine has evaporated.

2 Remove from the heat and add the sour cream, crab meat, fresh breadcrumbs, Parmesan, mustard, seasoning and chili paste. Mix well.

3 Cook the pasta shells in a large pan of boiling, salted water until *al dente*. Drain well, then arrange upside-down on a clean dish towel to dry.

4 Put the cream cheese, milk, ground paprika and mustard into a small pan. Heat gently and whisk until smooth. Season to taste.

5 Preheat the oven to 425°F. Fill the pasta shells with the crab mixture, spoon the cheese sauce into a shallow ovenproof dish and arrange the shells on top.

6 Mix together the dried bread crumbs and Parmesan cheese and sprinkle over the shells. Cover the dish with foil and bake for 15 minutes. Uncover and return to the oven for 5 minutes more. Serve at once.

NUTRITIONAL NOTES
PER PORTION:

ENERGY 514 calories **FAT** 8.8g
SATURATED FAT 3.5g **CHOLESTEROL** 79mg
CARBOHYDRATE 75g **FIBER** 3.3g

Penne with Spinach

Serves 4

INGREDIENTS
8 ounces fresh spinach
1 garlic clove, crushed
1 shallot or small onion,
   finely chopped
$1/2$ small red bell pepper, seeded and
   finely chopped
1 small red chili, seeded
   and chopped
$2/3$ cup stock
12 ounces penne
5 ounces smoked turkey bacon
3 tablespoons low-fat sour cream
2 tablespoons grated
   Parmesan cheese
shavings of Parmesan cheese,
   to garnish

red bell pepper

grated Parmesan cheese

red chilies

shallot

smoked turkey bacon

penne

stock

low-fat sour cream

garlic

spinach

1 Wash the spinach and remove the hard central stems. Shred finely.

2 Put the garlic, shallot or small onion, pepper and chili into a large frying pan. Add the stock, cover and cook for about 5 minutes until tender. Add the prepared spinach and cook quickly for another 2–3 minutes until it has wilted.

3 Cook the pasta in a large pan of boiling, salted water until *al dente*. Drain thoroughly.

4 Fry the smoked turkey bacon, cool a little, and chop finely.

5 Stir the sour cream and grated Parmesan into the pasta with the spinach, and toss carefully together.

6 Transfer to serving plates and sprinkle with chopped turkey and shavings of Parmesan cheese.

NUTRITIONAL NOTES
PER PORTION:

ENERGY 422 calories **FAT** 6.8g
SATURATED FAT 3.2g **CHOLESTEROL** 38mg
CARBOHYDRATE 71g **FIBER** 4.4g

Tagliatelle with Milanese Sauce

Serves 4

INGREDIENTS

1 onion, finely chopped
1 stalk celery, finely chopped
1 red bell pepper, seeded and diced
1–2 garlic cloves, crushed
²/₃ cup vegetable stock
14 ounce can tomatoes
1 tbsp tomato paste
2 teaspoons sugar
1 teaspoon mixed dried herbs
12 ounces tagliatelle
4 ounces button mushrooms, sliced
4 tablespoons white wine
4 ounces lean cooked ham, diced
salt and ground black pepper
1 tablespoon chopped fresh parsley,
    to garnish

garlic

celery

tagliatelle

red pepper

onion

lean cooked ham

button mushrooms

parsley

tomato paste

vegetable stock

tomatoes

white wine

1 Put the chopped onion, celery, pepper and garlic into a non-stick pan. Add the stock, bring to a boil and cook for 5 minutes or until tender.

2 Add the tomatoes, tomato paste, sugar and herbs. Season with salt and pepper. Bring to a boil, simmer for 30 minutes until thick. Stir occasionally.

3 Cook the pasta in a large pan of boiling, salted water until *al dente*. Drain thoroughly.

4 Put the mushrooms into a pan with the white wine, cover and cook for 3–4 minutes until tender and all the wine has evaporated.

5 Add the mushrooms and diced ham to the tomato sauce. Reheat gently.

6 Transfer the pasta to a warmed serving dish and spoon on the sauce. Garnish with parsley.

NUTRITIONAL NOTES

PER PORTION:

ENERGY 405 calories **FAT** 3.5g
SATURATED FAT 0.8g **CHOLESTEROL** 17mg
CARBOHYDRATE 77g **FIBER** 4.5g

INDEX